Charting Your
Family's Course

Charting Your Family's Course

ERIC BUEHRER

While this book is intended for the
reader's personal enjoyment and profit,
it is also designed for group study. A
personal and group study guide is located at the end of this text.

VICTOR BOOKS

A DIVISION OF SCRIPTURE PRESS PUBLICATIONS INC.
USA CANADA ENGLAND

Copyediting: Barbara Williams, Greg Clouse
Cover Design: Joe DeLeon
Group Study Guide: Gary Wilde

Library of Congress Cataloging-in-Publication Data

Buehrer, Eric.
    Charting your family's course / by Eric Buehrer.
       p.   cm.
    ISBN 0-89693-977-4
    1. Family — Religious life. 2. Family. 3. Children — Religious life.
4. Children — Conduct of life. I. Title.
    BV4526.2.B79 1992
    248.8'45 — dc20   91-39477
                                                CIP

CONTENTS

DEDICATION

To my wife Kim, the joy of my life: friend, lover, encourager, and helpmate—without whom this book would simply not have been written.

And on her lover's arm she leant,

And round her waist she felt it fold,

And far across the hills they went

In that new world which is the old.

—Tennyson

ACKNOWLEDGMENTS

There are many people whom I'd like to thank for making this book possible: Dr. Robert Simonds for his insight; Ben Gieringer for the many hours of discussion and help in crafting many of the principles contained in the book; Lee La Jeunesse for his advice on learning styles; Gene Bedley (National PTA Educator of the Year for 1985) for his help in understanding elementary kids; Dr. Bill Knight for his comments on self-image; Dr. Michelle McCormack for her insight on children's emotional needs; and, Dr. Arnold Burron for his enthusiastic support and confidence in this project.

INTRODUCTION

"Achievement," "Success," "Fulfillment," those are things we all strive to have. The Apostle Paul wrote that he "pressed on" to reach the high calling. Constantly he talked of "laboring" in his ministry.

Proverbs 13:4 states, "The soul of the sluggard desireth, and hath nothing; but the soul of the diligent shall be made fat" (KJV).

Proverbs 22:29 says, "Seest thou a man diligent in his business? He shall stand before kings" (KJV).

Yet, Solomon, the wisest man on the face of the earth, looked back on his life full of achievements, successes, and fulfillments, and in the Book of Ecclesiastes he says with despair, "Then I looked on all the works that my hands had wrought, and on the labor that I had labored to do: and, behold, all was vanity and vexation of spirit, and there was no profit under the sun" (2:11, KJV).

So what *is* success? What *is* achievement? This book is designed to address those questions. It is about strategic living—living life on purpose. The principles covered in the book can be applied to anyone: employees, spouses, friends, and colleagues. Specifically, we will look at how to apply these concepts to children. We will focus on how to help your child achieve academically, emotionally, spiritually, and morally.

Living Your Life on Purpose

> *Navigating Principle #1:* You, as a parent, are the first and most influential teacher in the lives of your children.

One of the most important ingredients for finding satisfaction with life is having a sense of purpose. To know that your life is contributing to "the bigger picture" or to feel that you are right where God wants you to be creates a wonderful feeling of contentment. Some people describe it as "running on all eight cylinders" or "being in the groove." Your talents are used fully in contributing toward a definable life goal. When people ask you what you are doing with your life, you answer confidently and decisively about your direction. That's living life on purpose. When you carry that sense of purpose into your family, you are experiencing strategic family living.

Let's face it, many of us live life by accident. We backed into our jobs. We stumbled into our marriage. We don't plan farther ahead than this year's vacation. We are not

sure what our talents are. We just hope that our kids
grow up to reach their "potential." But we aren't sure
what that is and we are keenly aware that we certainly
haven't reached ours.

That can all change. You can be sure of your talents.
You can specifically define areas of life for which God has
equipped you. You can pursue your dreams with confidence and you can show your children how to do that
too. In short, you *can* live life on purpose, rather than by
accident. Charting your family's course means thinking
about where you are right now in life, where you want to
go, and how to get there little by little each day.

The first principle in navigating your family's ship
across uncertain waters is vitally important. You are the
first and most influential teacher in the lives of your
children. *You can* make a tremendous impact on your
children's lives. If you get nothing else from this book get
this: You can provide your children with the tools to
succeed in life spiritually, morally, and academically.
School, television, magazines, and peers all play a part in
a child's development. But you are the most influential
factor of all. You can help your children live life on
purpose.

Many parents assume that the school will teach their
child how to achieve in life. Too much weight is put on
the ability of schools to transform children. Though
many good teachers have tremendous impact on children
each day, in the end it will be the active work of Mom
and Dad that determines what kind of head start that
child will have.

Consider this: By the time a child reaches the sixth
grade he or she will have spent about 6,000 hours at
school and about 60,000 hours at home. So, just in
hours, the home has ten times the influence over the
school. And of course, because the early developmental
years of the child are spent at home almost exclusively,
what happens in the home is crucial in helping a child
achieve.

MEDIOCRE EDUCATION THREATENS YOUR CHILD

Though your child spends many more hours at home than he does at school, his time at school has tremendous impact on him. Children are increasingly threatened by a rising tide of mediocrity in school. I was in Erie, Pennsylvania presenting a workshop when a father approached me about his son. He showed me a two-page history report his tenth-grade son had turned in to the teacher. The teacher had returned the paper having marked it with an 'A' and written the comments, "Good report, very interesting and well written." Rather than being proud, the father was despondent. He showed me why. In this two-page report with only eighty-one lines of typed text there were 144 spelling, punctuation, and grammatical errors! "I'm at home trying to motivate my son to do well while the school is rewarding him for failure!" he said. I asked him the teacher's response on seeing the father's red marks all over the report. "The teacher was unconcerned about it and said he was merely trying to help my son's self-esteem."

Academic mediocrity is the scholastic disease that is sweeping our nation. *Time* magazine captured its essence in an article entitled, "Education = Doing Bad and Feeling Good" (February 5, 1990). The article points out that on one international math test American students ranked last and Koreans ranked first. But when the same students' self-esteem was tested the Koreans said they felt they were the worst in math. You guessed it, the American students ranked themselves highest in evaluating their own ability in math.

From the mid-1960s to the 1980s national Scholastic Aptitude Test scores dropped an average of forty points in math and over fifty points in verbal skills.

In comparing American students to others around the world it was found that on nineteen academic tests, American children were never first or second and were ranked last seven times.

The number of illiterate Americans increases by 2.5 million each year. When you exclude immigrants which make up slightly more than half that figure, you're left with more than 1 million illiterate children coming from our school system.

A 1975 study by the University of Texas found that one out of five of the 15,000 people tested could not write a check without an error so great that a bank could not cash it. Twenty-two percent could not address an envelope well enough to ensure delivery by the post office. An incredible four out of every ten people could not figure correct change from a store purchase.

Insight magazine reported that when Dallas, Texas high school students were asked to name the country which borders the United States to the south, nearly one out of three students could not do so.

In a survey done by the Hearst Corporation, 45 percent of those Americans polled thought that Karl Marx's phrase "from each according to his ability, to each according to his need" is in the U.S. Constitution. A 1987 study, based on a survey funded by the National Endowment for the Humanities, reported that more than two-thirds of the nation's seventeen-year-olds are unable to locate the Civil War within the correct half-century!

During a presentation in Fort Myers, Florida a mother told me why she is now home schooling her eighth-grade daughter. The girl was getting good marks in school—A's and B's. But when the mother had her tested independent of the school district she discovered that her daughter was functioning at the fifth-grade level.

But the need for higher achievement and more successful living is not found just in academics. From 1950 to 1979 serious crimes committed by children increased 11,000 percent. Half the burglars arrested in America are under eighteen years old. What's more, alarming numbers of young people are among the grim statistics of alcoholism, suicide, unwed mothers, abortions, and runaways.

Are children in need of solid tools with which they can become achievers? Whether we look at their need academically, morally, emotionally, or spiritually, the answer is an obvious yes.

MEDIOCRE ACHIEVERS
Lawrence Greene, the founder of The Development Learning Center, estimates that 50 percent of all school-age children are underachievers. That means that you very likely have underachieving children.

Before you panic, it's important to look at what I mean by "an underachieving child." Your child can be very bright—a good student—but still be *under*achieving. A student who is capable of making straight A's but who only works hard enough to get B's is an underachiever. A person with great athletic ability but who is lazy about the way he or she pursues that ability is an underachiever. With that in mind, let's look at some aspects of underachievers.

Common characteristics of underachievers are such things as:

1. A general dislike for themselves. They put themselves down and feel they have very little worth.
2. A lack of self-confidence. They have lost faith in their ability to achieve.
3. A shirking of responsibility.
4. A penchant for doing assignments at the last minute. You can never get an underachiever to turn something in on time. And he drives you crazy because he can never seem to break out of that pattern.
5. A tendency to do a minimum amount of homework. You know how that one goes: "How's your homework goin'?" (child): "Fine." (parent): "Did you finish your reading?" (child): "Yeah." But somehow you have a sneaking suspicion that though his eyes looked at the pages, his brain was dreaming up the

plot to the next Steven Spielberg movie.

You can have a very bright child, fun loving, and active
but still have an underachiever on your hands.

The Bible says in Proverbs 22:6 that we are to "train a
child in the way he should go, and when he is old he will
not turn from it." This can be looked at two different
ways, each having value. We are to both train a child in
the way he *should* go and the way *he* should go. There
are certain things a child ought to do. There are particular moral, spiritual, and academic qualities a child *should*
have. Also important is the individuality of each child.
God has given each of us unique talents and interests
that He expects us to use for His glory. Thus, we are to
train a child in the way *he* should go instead of the way
we wish he would go.

Another important aspect of that verse in Proverbs is
the idea of training. Training involves more than merely
telling someone something. It involves coaching, evaluating, guiding, teaching, disciplining, and encouraging. For
instance, to think that a child will automatically grow up
well-grounded spiritually because you take him to church
each week is like thinking he'll become a good athlete by
going to the stadium once a week and jogging once
around the track.

A good athlete requires hours of intense training, a
regimen, a coach who evaluates him and pushes him to
improvement. He must practice, practice, practice. He
has goals that he pushes himself toward.

When we are getting ready to launch our family on its
voyage through life we would do well to remember the
sailor's poem:

There was once an old sailor my grandfather knew,
Who had so many things which he wanted to do.
But whenever he thought it was time to begin,
He couldn't because of the fog he was in.

To break out of the "fog" you may be in, you must

take three vital steps. You must evaluate your family's present location in life; you must chart your family's course; and you must guide your family on its voyage.

THE TOOLS FOR YOUR VOYAGE

Setting out on a voyage is a good metaphor for life. Everywhere we look there are storm clouds and reefs on the horizon ready to sink the ship of your family. Whether it is in the academic, moral, emotional, or spiritual areas, rough waters lie ahead. God has placed you at the helm of your family's ship. He has provided you with the sextant, chart, and compass for your voyage through life.

On the sea the *sextant* is used to locate your present position. It's that triangular shaped instrument captains use to figure out where they are. So it is in charting your family's course. Before determining how to get where you want to go you must first figure out where you are. The *chart* shows you the course you are to follow to reach your destination. Every captain has many charts that correspond to the part of the world in which he is sailing. By using the sextant and the chart he can determine where he is, where he wants to go, and the best path to get there. The *compass* is used to know the direction you must go in order to reach your destination. Every ship is equipped with a compass. It is one thing to have your destination plotted on a chart and quite another thing to know which way to steer your ship to correspond with the chart. The captain can lay the chart on his table with north pointing toward the ship's galley. But he must then know which direction to point the bow of the ship in order to also be pointing north. That requires a compass. Many mid-course corrections are needed and frequent use of all three instruments is important. God has given us the Bible, His Holy Spirit, and common sense to know where we are in life, where we should be going, and the best path to get there.

Picture the wheel of a ship. You are at that wheel steering the direction of your own life and also your fam-

ily's. God is at the center of the wheel. His principles are
the hub on which all else pivots. The day-to-day areas of
life such as education, vocation, finances, recreation, and
spiritual development form the handles on the outer rim
of the wheel. There is one thing we often forget: We must
turn the wheel to get where we should go. We must manage God's divine principles working out through the various areas of our lives. Everything pivots around God's
Word, but the Bible is clear that we are held responsible
for how we manage our time, energies, attitudes, and
resources. For instance, God has said that laziness is
wrong. That principle forms an important "hub" in our
wheel. But how each person manages that principle in
his or her life will be different. God may call one person
to be a doctor and that person must go through many
years of medical school. Another person is called to be a
teacher and only has to go through five years of college.
Is the teacher lazy for not pursuing a doctoral degree?
No, the teacher has properly managed the call of God.
But the person called to be a doctor would be lazy if,
through lack of diligent application, he did not go to medical school. God directs, but we manage. When we manage our energies and abilities unwisely we may find ourselves out of the will of God. When we don't understand
our proper role as managers of our lives under God's
direction He does things *in spite of us* rather than
through us.

ANCHORING STRATEGIES
You are the most influential teachers in the life of your
children. It is vital that key principles of life be anchored
in your children's hearts. Each of the twelve navigating
principles outlined in this book can be anchored in your
children's lives by answering three questions. At the end
of each chapter the three anchoring questions are asked
and examples are given. I highly recommend that you
ponder how you will answer each question for each of
your children

The first anchoring question is, "What do I teach to my child?" Teaching involves giving knowledge to your child on how to navigate life's waters. After learning the principle outlined in each chapter, ask yourself what (and how) you will teach about that principle to your child.

The second question is, "How do I model it for my child?" Modeling for your child means demonstrating successful ways to navigate life's waters. Your child will imitate the way you do things. He or she will develop the attitudes and habits you model. After you have read the success principles in each chapter, ask yourself how you will model that principle to your child.

Modeling successful habits for your child means that you have a loving relationship with your child; let your child see how you came to make a particular principle part of your life; let your child observe you practicing the principle in your life; share with your child what you are thinking and feeling; be consistent in your behavior and values.

The third question is, "What do I encourage in my child?" Encouraging your child means instilling confidence in his or her ability to be successful in navigating life's waters. The word *encourage* has as its root the Latin word *cor,* meaning "heart." To be *dis*couraged is to lose heart. To be *en*couraged is to inspire with hope and confidence; to hearten.

When you encourage someone, especially your child, you are strengthening his confidence to move forward successfully. Encouragement brings out the inner qualities your child possesses. To be an encourager is to say, "Look what you have inside you! That's great! Now, keep going because I believe in your ability to overcome this obstacle!" Even in spiritual matters, being an encourager is to remind a person of the words of God hidden in the heart and say, "Look what God has given (grace, forgiveness, spiritual blessings, etc.)! That's great! Don't lose heart. Instead, by faith, hold on to that and overcome this obstacle."

When asking the third question: "What do I encourage in my child?" think about the principle covered in the chapter you just read and determine how your child may already be living out a part of that good principle. Then, encourage your child to do it more.

SUMMARY

The first navigating principle in preparing for life's voyage with your family is: You are the first and most influential teacher in the lives of your children. Take confidence in your ability to guide them to success. They look up to you more than to anyone else. Because of the mediocrity that surrounds us all—especially in the public schools—it is vitally important that you begin thinking strategically where you want your family to be in a few years and how you are going to get there. God is the center of your life around whom all things pivot, but He expects you to manage your life using the talents, time, opportunities and energies He uniquely gave you. As you begin to steer your family on its voyage, remember to ask yourself three questions that enable you to consciously influence the lives of your children: what do I teach to my child, how do I model for my child, and what do I encourage in my child?

Anchoring Questions for Chapter One:

1. What will you teach to your child about living life on purpose?

2. How will you model living life on purpose for your child in the next sixty days?
   Example: I will set a goal to get a book from the library on the same subject my child is learning about at school and make sure she sees me reading it at home. I will model what I believe about education being important.

3. What will I encourage in my child?

Example: I notice my child likes to play baseball and has practiced hard to make the Little League team. I will encourage the qualities of hard work, diligence, and his careful planning in pursuing a goal.

Boost Your Child's
Self-image Biblically

Navigating Principle #2: Your lifestyle is based on your self-image which is formed by your relationship with God.

Your life reflects your relationship with God. Everyone has some type of relationship with God. Many people have a hostile one. The Bible refers to it as enmity between God and man. Others, at least, have a healthy relationship with God because they have come to Him through Jesus Christ. Still others have a wonderfully intimate walk with Him.

How you live your life each day is based on how you see yourself—your self-image. Are you a winner? Do you have abilities that God is using? Or are you pessimistic? Do you dwell on the negative in yourself? Listen to the wonderful things God has said are at your fingertips just waiting to be used: "I will never leave you or forsake you" (Josh. 1:5). "The Lord is my strength" (Ps. 28:7). "I can do everything through Him who gives me strength" (Phil. 4:13), "Be anxious for nothing" (v. 6, NASB).

A non-Christian sees his life without God. His identity is one of lonely self-reliance. He believes that only the human things around him shape who he is. His lifestyle will reflect that perspective. He may chase after material wealth in seeking to define who he is. He may excessively cling to human relationships because only in those earthly connections does he feel a sense of worth. In short, he lives his life each day thinking only of himself.

Many Christians act just like unbelievers because they do not apply God's words to their lives. Though they have the foundation to enjoy being a truly fulfilled human as God intended, they never build on that foundation. They never take the words of God into their minds. They never make it so much a part of their thinking that they can enjoy the "peace which passes all understanding" (see Phil. 4:7). This results in anxiety and lack of confidence that cripples any progress toward success in many areas of life.

In the earthly arena, we gain a sense of who we are by looking at our reflection found in the feedback we receive from others. If someone consistently tells us we lack talent or vice versa, we will often internalize that feedback and shape our identity accordingly.

Our relationship with God is similar. As Christians we can gain a sense of who we are by looking at what our Heavenly Father "feeds back" to us. We often listen to what mere men are saying about us with a more attentive ear than we listen to God. This results in a distorted view of ourselves and our priorities, and true happiness can never occur.

YOU AND YOUR CHILDREN ARE UNIQUE

Understanding our uniqueness is important in shaping who we are. In talking to children we can point out that there are several things that show us who we are. Outwardly, we can look at our thumbprints, our voices, our silhouettes, or our pictures. These are physical things that show our uniqueness. You can help children see their individuality by using an ink pad and some paper to compare fingerprints. Use an audio tape recorder to have fun discovering how each person has a unique sound to his voice. These outward things come from the creative hand of God.

We also can discover our inward uniqueness. We can look at the thoughts and feelings God has given us. No one thinks exactly alike. God has given us each a brain and the ability to think. Identical twins may seem exactly alike, but not in their thoughts. God has given us each a unique personality and has set each of us on a unique path of growth. No one shares the same experiences God brings. You and your children are unique!

It is never too late to reverse your child's low self-image. The foundation of solid self-perception can be repaired, rebuilt, or demolished at any time during your child's life. Studies have shown that your talking and reactions to your child play a fundamental role in shaping his or her basic attitudes. Researchers at Stanford University found, for instance, that how parents reacted to their kids' report cards affected the student's overall performance. If parents expressed disapproval and disappointment, the children became discouraged and their achievement went down. If the parents showed little interest in their children's grades, again, the children's achievement went down.

The children who achieved best were those whose parents showed interest, praised good work, and encouraged better performance where the children did poorly. The parents let the children know that they were there to help if needed.

You are the most significant people in your child's life whether your child tells you that or not. How you respond to your child is important in the formation of his or her self-image. Achievement thrives best in an environment of security. When a child feels secure, he can risk venturing out knowing that failure will not jeopardize his standing with his parents.

A BIBLICAL VIEW OF SELF-IMAGE

There are those Christians today who downplay the importance of theology (the study of God). It doesn't seem as practical as such topics as how to have a happy marriage or how to be financially free. We are more interested today in the product of the Christian life than the perspective of the Christian life. To use the old saying, that is putting the cart before the horse. The right perspective will lead to the right production. But if we only strive for the production we will be tempted to use any means at our disposal to get there. We may fall back on humanly devised approaches to overcoming a problem and have the appearance of victory. After a while the shallowness of our "solution" becomes apparent and we chase after the next seemingly great idea on how to solve our problems.

It is important to our self-image that we grow in our understanding of God's perspective on life. Such study is theological. It is studying about God. It is from an encounter with God that we find who we are. But because of our lack of faith, we turn to the encounters with fellow humans who themselves are trying to find happiness. It is like trying to get a healthy view of life by choosing an emotionally disturbed mentor rather than the most balanced and fulfilled Mentor in the universe. Important in helping children develop healthy self-images is helping them understand how God sees them.

Our Heavenly Father is the perfect Parent. He has given us wonderfully encouraging feedback on who we are and what we can do in life. He gives us a secure world and always seeks what is best for us. The more we open our ears to what He is saying to us, the more we read the words He has written to us, the more we will benefit by having a healthy, biblical self-image. If we base our self-image on things or people who always change, our self-image will vacillate too. By basing our self-image on God, who never changes, our self-image can grow in stability even as we grow in our understanding of God.

WHAT GOD SAYS ABOUT YOU

Take a look at just a few things God has said about you that provide the basis for a wonderfully healthy self-image.

You were specially chosen to be in God's plan.	Ephesians 1:11
You do not have your sins counted against you.	2 Corinthians 5:19
You have been redeemed by Christ's sacrifice.	1 Peter 1:18-19
You have a tremendous destiny with God.	Colossians 3:4
You have direct and open access to God.	Ephesians 2:18
You are the object of His special love.	Ephesians 2:4
You are guided by His unique plan.	Philippians 2:13
You are uniquely protected by God each day.	Psalm 37:23-24
You have unusual powers through prayer.	James 5:15-16

This list represents only a few of the many things we have from God. As you understand more and more about the wonderful blessings God has bestowed on you, a uniquely Christian self-image will begin to shine in your heart. There are many factors that develop a healthy self-image from a biblical perspective, but two stand out: God created us and God redeemed us. Everything else is derived from those two facts.

GOD CREATED YOUR CHILD

God created us in His image. He made us like Him in that we can think, organize, plan, create, build, manage, lead, feel, love, give, and do many other things. When we are doing any of those things that God created us to do, we are bringing glory to Him.

Psalm 19:1 tells us, "The heavens declare the glory of God; the skies proclaim the work of His hands." The stars and the planets don't do anything extraordinary. They don't do anything beyond what God created them to do. They just sit there. But by doing what God created them to do they are glorifying Him.

The same is true for you. When you do what God created you to do you are bringing glory to Him. What abilities has He given you? What opportunities has He placed in front of you? No two people's abilities or opportunities are the same. When you simply do what God has given you to do, you glorify Him. A person who has been gifted to manage and who manages well is glorifying God. An artist or musician who exhibits the talents God has given him or her is glorifying God.

There are two levels we can talk about when referring to glorifying God as His creatures. First, the mere fact of our creation brings Him glory. The incredible intricacy of the human body humbles us to worship Him. A very basic building block for constructing a healthy self-image is a simple recognition of how wonderfully He made us. In our bodies, all the cells work together every second of our lives. That is amazing! When we get sick, the body can often heal itself. It is amazing that all the cells and all the organs can function harmoniously for even one second let alone for eighty or ninety years.

We can each feel good about how God has made us because He *chose* to make us that way. Are you considered "ugly" by the world's standards? Do you think God made a mistake? Maybe He didn't know what He was doing when He fashioned you in your mother's womb? God doesn't make mistakes. One poster of a little boy reads, "I know I'm somebody 'cause God don't make junk." What a simple, yet profound phrase.

You may have a poor self-image about your looks be-

cause you are seeking your image in the wrong mirror.
Stop dwelling on the mirror in your bathroom and start
looking intently in God's mirror. He says you are "fear-
fully and wonderfully made" (Ps. 139:14), and "Man
looks at the outward appearance, but the Lord looks at
the heart" (1 Sam. 16:7), and "Stop judging by mere
appearances" (John 7:24).

On one level you can increase your self-image by realizing that you are special just for *being* His creation. On
another level you can enhance your self-image by *doing*
what He created you to do. As God's creature, whenever
you do what God created you to do you are, to one degree
or another, glorifying Him. I say to one degree or another
because you must show some initiative to do what He
created you to do. To the degree that you work in that
area you glorify Him.

We have fallen prey to the idea that if you are a Christian who has artistic ability you can only glorify God by
painting Christian bumper stickers. If you are a musician
and a Christian you *must* write songs with Christian
words or you are not glorifying God. Nothing could be
further from the truth. Such logic would require the
manager to use his management skills only in a ministry.
A carpenter could only use his talent building churches.
A mechanic could only work on missionaries' cars. Anything else would not bring glory to God.

Just as your body shows the creative power of God and
is testimony to Him, so your God-given abilities show His
handiwork and, when used, are a testimony to Him. You
don't have to tattoo your body with Gospel messages in
order for God to be praised. Neither do you need to "tattoo" your abilities with Gospel slogans to glorify God in
your life.

GOD REDEEMED YOUR CHILD

The second important factor in creating a biblical self-
image is to recognize that God redeemed us (assuming
you have placed your faith in Christ). Psychologists talk

about the importance of unconditional love in shaping the self-image. The Bible has explained this all along Romans 5:8 states, "But God demonstrates His own love for us in this: While we were still sinners, Christ died for us." Nothing we could *do* would be good enough to deserve Christ sacrificing His life for us. He died for us unconditionally while we were still hopelessly lost in sin.

Since God is a Spirit, having a relationship with God is spiritual. That means we must connect with Him spiritually. Yet, it is amazing how many people try to *do* something physically to gain His favor. Nothing we could do physically, such as give to the poor or abstain from certain food, could ever gain favor with God. Instead, we must connect with God spiritually and there is only one thing a human being can do to touch the spiritual dimension: express faith.

Why is God's redemption of us so important for a healthy self-image? For two reasons: first, we are to love one another (including our kids) like Jesus loved the church—unconditionally and sacrificially; and second, as the recipients of God's love and perfect righteousness we are members of the royal family. The King is our Father. We are His sons and daughters. We now have access to tremendous spiritual blessings because of this new position. We have all these blessings for simply being, not doing. His unconditional love provides us with all we need. He forgives us, He accepts us, and He blesses us.

Our value doesn't come from mere existence. That is what the secularists cling to and is why they look to themselves for esteem. Our value comes from a gracious declaration from God. Without God's gracious favor shown to humans we would have no greater value to God than rocks, trees, or ants. This, at first, may seem to be a blow to our self-image. It is, actually, the greatest boost to our self-image we could ever imagine! Instead of looking inward for some kind of intrinsic worth, we are to look to God who, by grace, gave us worth. If we trust in how *we* feel about our worth, our self-image will go up and down with the highs and lows of our emotions. But since God is the ultimate authority on all things, has the final word about all things, and never changes, our self-worth is established in the bedrock of God's own character. We can have a good self-image because we are now related to the King of kings through His grace. No matter what you've done in your past the Bible says we are new creations at salvation. Old things have "passed away." God doesn't hold your former sins up to shame you. Now that should do wonders for your self-image!

Self-image refers to how we see ourselves. Having been redeemed by God we need to see ourselves as blessed with every spiritual blessing heaven has to offer. Dozens of things were given to us by God at salvation including such things as access to Him in prayer, the indwelling of His Holy Spirit, and the security of being considered by God to be in Christ and thereby, secure in salvation.

We, as Christians, now have a spirit alive to God's indwelling Spirit. We are therefore able to interact with God regularly, and have available to us all the blessings of heaven. To the degree that we understand this, we enhance our self-image. God has, since the dawn of time, proclaimed this truth that affects human emotion. More recently, cognitive psychology has "modernized" this principle. Christian psychologist Dr. William Backus points out, "It is the content of human thinking that makes the difference between misery and happiness. What matters is not the event, but how a person appraises and evaluates the event. What occurs outside him does not make him joyful or wretched, angry or benevolent, peaceful or turbulent. What he *believes* about the event makes all the difference."

SELF-ESTEEM VERSUS SELF-IMAGE

The matter of esteem is all the rage now in both secular and Christian circles. In California some legislators and educators refer to self-esteem training as the "social vaccine" which will cure crime, drug use, teen pregnancy, and all other social ills. Unfortunately, such thinking rests on the faulty assumption that if a person feels good about himself he will act virtuously. Self-esteem is confused with morality. This thinking filters into the classroom with all kinds of exercises that actually promote self-centeredness rather than healthy views of the self.

One classroom activity, for instance, has the teacher hold up a paper bag and tell the kids that in the bag is the *most* important thing in the world. Everyone is to try to guess what is in the bag. Finally, the teacher reaches in the bag and pulls out a mirror. The message is, "You are the most important thing in the world." This artificial pumping up of the self creates an unstable foundation for a child's self-esteem. If he is consistently raised on such a premise, he will spend the rest of his life investing himself in things which reinforce that he is the most important thing in the world (before God, country, family, community, or *his* own kids).

On the other hand, many Christians are guilty of swinging too far the opposite direction and promoting the defeated image. These people hang their head (I assume they think they are being humble) and say, "I am nothing and can't do anything." After church you may approach the pianist who has a defeated image. When you compliment her on her playing she states, "Oh, it wasn't me." Surprised, you explain that you have 20-20 vision and thought for sure you saw her playing the piano. "It was the Lord," she corrects you. You find yourself wanting to say, "If it was the Lord, why were you practicing three hours a day for the last week?"

For some of us, playing the piano at church truly would require a miracle from the Lord. If I played the piano well enough to lead the congregation in singing I could honestly say it was the Lord playing and not me. It would have to be! Does that sound irreverent to you? Maybe you are suffering from a defeated image.

What is the balance between esteeming yourself too much or too little? It is recognizing that God has given

you incredible talents, abilities, and opportunities that
He expects you to manage in His service and by His
power. Yes, they are from God. But you must invest time
and energy to bring them out. God may have gifted you
with musical ability but your laziness quenches that talent. Your diligence can bring out the talent and opportunities God has given you. As you increase the skills God
has given you, your self-image will begin to soar!

A PHYSICAL LOOK AT SELF-IMAGE
There is a physiological aspect to self-image. Brain researchers have found what is called the reticular activating system. It is located in the cerebral cortex of the
brain and acts like a gatekeeper for stimuli flowing to the
brain. If your brain never filtered all the signals coming
from your five senses, your system would overload. Every
second of your life your brain is receiving stimuli from
your sight, touch, taste, smell, and hearing.

When, for instance, your eyes are open they are seeing
thousands, even millions of combinations of colors and
shapes simultaneously. Your body is constantly using its
sense of touch to monitor every inch of your body for
pain or discomfort—not only on the outside, but on the
inside as well.

The reticular activating system acts as a filter for the
brain so it can concentrate on that which it deems important. It prioritizes stimuli based on three things: our
needs, our goals, and our self-image. When you need
something such as food or warmth, nerves send a signal
to the brain and you then can act to relieve the discomfort. If you have a goal of, for instance, finding a particular recipe in a card file, you can thumb through dozens of
cards very quickly until your eye "locks on" the object of
your search. Your brain sees the other cards but filters
them out while searching for the right card. If you are in
sales and have a particular financial goal, your brain
keeps you on the lookout for opportunities to fulfill that
goal. Many irrelevant opportunities pass before you each

day, but your reticular activating system opens and
closes based on your goal of reaching a particular financial goal.

Your self-image also determines when your gatekeeper
will open and close. You may enjoy singing but have
always been told you can't carry a tune in a bucket. One
day, while singing at church, a friend comments that you
have a nice voice and should consider the choir. What
does your brain do with that compliment? It rejects it!
The statement never gets past the reticular activating
system. And you end up insulting your friend by quickly
informing him that you have a terrible voice and could
never consider the choir. Your self-image helped set the
priorities for your gatekeeper. Consequently, you never
notice the opportunities for singing in the choir or join-
ing the local civic musical production. Things that, deep
inside, you know you would love to do but, as you say to
yourself, can't.

Think of the misleading self-images we reinforce: "I'm
no good at math," "I never could sing," "I'm just not a
public speaker." So, you miss opportunities God places
before you. He may have given you an ability and a desire
for something that got quenched at an early age. Don't
do the same thing to your children. Many times a parent
may try to protect a child from the disappointment of
failure by steering him away from an opportunity. The
unintentional message over time to that child is clear:
"You shouldn't try because you can't be successful."

THE FIVE GREAT TRUTHS

Flowing from a healthy relationship with God comes five
great truths. These truths provide stability and motivation to our lives. They become the means to spiritual,
moral, physical, social, and economic success.

1. I have value and worth. The source of our value
and worth flows from what God has done. He created
each of us in His image and likeness. He has given us
new life through redemption.

It is important for us to have an accurate view or opinion of our worth and value. We need to think neither too much nor too little of ourselves but recognize who we are in Christ. A person's value and worth do not come from achievement or possessions but from a relationship with God through Jesus Christ.

2. I have a purpose. Most people in the world have no sense of purpose. Dying with "the most toys" is the highest ideal of some people. Yet, the Christian has the purpose of being conformed to God's image, loving and serving Him, being obedient to His commands, serving others, and bringing a godly influence to every aspect of life.

Having a purpose helps us answer why we should develop our talents and abilities. We never know when God will use us. He may need to pass us over because even though He gave us the ability to do a particular task in His service, we never took the time or made the effort to develop that area.

Even more specifically, we need to seek to find our personal purpose in life. Doug Bradley, an expert in time management and life planning, is fond of asking, "What do you bring to the party of life?" Years ago over dinner he challenged me to establish a specific purpose in life. We often think in generalities when answering the question, "Why am I here?" We answer with something that could fit anyone: "To glorify God." But, why did God put *you* on this earth? Why at this time with the talents and opportunities you have? A life purpose is a wonderful tool for determining your life's direction.

Ask yourself what talents and abilities you have. What are three needs you have a burning desire to see met? This may be an area you think of often. Write some rough draft sentences that describe what you think your life purpose statement may be. Eventually, boil it down to one succinct paragraph that has three vital elements: "I help people (to do what?)"; "By (by what means do you help them?)"; "Which results in (what outcome?)."

Your life purpose statement is not cast in stone. It will change as you change. As you learn new things and have new experiences, your personal sense of mission will change. But, having something written down gives you a greater sense of what your purpose in life may be.

At the time of this writing my life purpose statement is: "I help people break through problems by bringing together a variety of ideas and blending them into a fresh approach which results in a new path toward success in understanding or applying biblical principles." The first half of the statement deals with unique skills that could apply to many environments. The second half of the statement focuses on what I feel called by God to do.

A life purpose statement is more than just knowing your spiritual gift. My spiritual gift is teaching. But not all teachers will teach with the same style. Some are good at one-on-one counseling; others are best when lecturing; and some are great at leading discussions. Having a life purpose statement helps narrow *how* you do what you do.

3. I have standards. God's Word clearly outlines a code of conduct for both society and for the Christian. By understanding my relationship to Him I can have standards by which to measure right and wrong.

In a society where right and wrong is now measured in one's subjective experience, God's standards act as an anchor to stabilize us in turbulent waters.

Christians are often ridiculed because we express one standard of moral conduct but often fail to live up to it. Such criticism is unfair. It is better to have a standard for which to strive, even though we may fail, than to have no standards just so we can feel good that we haven't violated anything. It is the establishment of standards that gives us the knowledge that we have sinned. A person with no objective standards never has a knowledge of wrong when there is no such thing as absolute right and wrong.

4. I have strength and confidence. Through God's

Holy Spirit living in us, we can have strength and confidence to meet life's challenges. The Apostle Paul says, "I can do all things through Him who strengthens me" (Phil. 4:13, NASB). The central message of the Bible is to trust God, to have confidence in His work in our lives both eternally and temporally. Everything in the Bible boils down to that simple message. Our courage (and courage is essential to success in anything) comes from faith in God. This is not just faith in His work of salvation, but faith in His moment-by-moment work in our lives. Such faith gives us confidence to live life boldly.

5. I have a hope and a destiny. Our hope is in Christ and our destiny is eternal life with Him. This fact gives us a fixed point by which we can handle the many trials and tests that come our way.

Henry David Thoreau said it well: Most men live lives of quiet desperation. Despair is an utter lack of hope. One reason people despair is because they lack any sense of destiny. They think, "What will all my toil ultimately result in?" A healthy relationship with God gives us a tremendous sense of hope because we know our destiny. We know that one day we will stand before our Lord and He will rebuke us or commend us on how we served Him in His power. This one great truth alone can do more to build your confidence to achieve here on earth than any other of the five great truths.

SUCCESS DEVELOPMENT

How does all this work in the practical, work-a-day-world? There are four stages for developing an attitude of success in your life. Once you have these stages clearly identified for yourself, you can teach them to your children and give them an early start on success. Do not despair if you have not actively moved through these four stages. There is still plenty of time.

The first stage is, as I said before, *a good relationship with God.* This forms the basis from which all else flows. The second stage which is directly related to your rapport with God is your *sense of purpose* in life. The stronger your walk with God, the stronger your sense of specific purpose. With a strong sense of purpose, you then can move into the third stage and have an *inner sense of well-being.* This is joy. You may not be happy with your circumstances, but you can have an inner sense of wellbeing that you are where God wants you to be. Finally, having gone through the first three stages you obtain *confidence.* Confidence is absolutely vital to achieving anything. Without it you won't even try anything. But confidence needs to be grounded in a solid foundation. The secular world tries to build up confidence with gimmicks. Looking in the mirror and repeating, "I am great, I can do it, I'm getting better" may have some temporal effect of pumping you up, but it lacks the solid foundation to adequately see you through setbacks.

Going through these four stages of success development gives you stability. Troubles come and knock you down, but not out. For a time, you may feel low, but never buried. You may need to retreat for a time to mend, but you won't need to retreat in surrender.

One day I was driving to work and began feeling down. Right there in my car I was having a little pity party. I began asking all kinds of questions of God about why I was doing what I was doing. Soon I found I had worked myself into a bad attitude. Then I stopped myself. I began asking questions that related to the four stages of success development. After some review, I felt I had a good relationship with God. When He led me to my particular job I felt a strong sense of calling. I had felt a peace about where He had moved me geographically. I could see His hand working in my life to bring greater opportunity to me. Certainly, with this in mind, I felt a strong sense of purpose. Then I asked, "If I feel God put me right where I am, why would I want to be anywhere else?" As I pondered that question a deep sense of wellbeing swept over me and I felt back on track in my confidence to proceed with the projects in which I was involved. I came to work with a spring in my step and a renewed freshness in my attitude.

These concepts can be taught to your children at an early age. How they live will be based on their view of themselves which is formed by the kind of relationship they have with God. This will form the bedrock for achievement in their lives. Whether it is in academics, spiritual growth, or moral development, your children can have a lifelong record of success.

SUMMARY

How you live your life is affected by what kind of relationship you have with God. Your identity—self-image—is grounded on two important biblical principles: God created you and God redeemed you. Everything else flows from that. Your child's self-image is also based on these two principles. This forms the foundation for true success in life. A healthy relationship with God leads to a sense of unique purpose which creates an inner sense of well-being. This, then, forms the foundation for having confidence to achieve in life.

Anchoring Questions for Chapter Two:

1. What will you teach your child about self-image this week?

2. What will you model in your life about a biblical self-image?

3. What has your child demonstrated about understanding a biblical self-image that you can encourage?

Define Biblical Success
for Your Child

➤————————————————————————————➤

Navigating Principal #3: Success is living in such a way
that you are using what God has given you—your intellect, abilities, and energies—to reach the purpose for
which He intended your life.

➤————————————————————————————➤

A n exciting adventure on the sea is recorded in Acts
27 when the Apostle Paul was shipwrecked while
on his way to Rome. Paul, from the start, warned
the sailors that the voyage across the Mediterranean
should not be made at that time because of stormy
weather. But the sailors decided to go anyway. While at
sea, a violent storm did indeed erupt. Paul had confidence in God's revealed purpose in his life and confidently declared that the crew and all the passengers would
survive the storm. At one point the crew tried to abandon ship. Paul used his intellect and energies to warn the
Roman centurion in charge, "Unless these men stay with
the ship, you cannot be saved." His confidence in God's
purpose in his life gave him the basis for providing comfort and leadership to the crew and all those aboard.
    A good working definition of success is especially im-

portant for healthy living in today's society. If you ask a
dozen people what success is, you will get twelve different answers. Some people measure success by money;
some measure it by position in life; some measure success by the relationships they have fostered; some measure it by comparing their accomplishments to those
around them.

A definition of success must be flexible enough to allow
for individuality while also being specific enough to dis-
tinguish it from failure. It does little good to define success so loosely that it becomes difficult to actually measure it. Often we do this as a way to boost our self-
esteem. Nobody wants to fail. So we sometimes define
success to come out winners in our current situation.
This is artificial self-esteem. Often this is expressed in
comments such as, "I feel good about where I am." That
may or may not be good. A "successful" criminal could
say that, but he is not successful in the broader sense of
the word. Subjective experience alone cannot be used to
measure success.

Success is relative to something. The man who mea-
sures success by money is never truly successful. He may
have a million dollars and, by his standards, be more
successful than a man who only has a thousand dollars.
However, he is a failure compared to the man with a
billion dollars!

The real question centers around how success is measured. It must be measured by some standard. The answer is that success is measured in relation to God. The
real question we must ask ourselves is what does He
want us to do in our lives. This is the age-old question
every Christian asks himself: "What is the will of God for
my life?"

Many good books have been written on the subject. In
the previous chapter I suggested a few ways to arrive at a
more specific awareness of God's will for your life. Rather than discuss that general subject at length here, let's
focus on the next step. Once you have a sense of God's

will for your life, how do you measure success in walking
in His will?

This brings us to our definition of success: *Success is
living in such a way that you are using what God has
given you—your intellect, abilities, and energies—to
reach the purpose for which He intended your life.*

Your children have many God-given abilities. They
have abilities to create, to build, to organize—in short, to
achieve. But God intends each person to use them differently. That is why success must always be measured in
relation to God's intention for each one of us.

Many times we can gain a clearer idea of what God's
will is by the opportunities He places before us. I'm reminded of my mother's advice when, as a teenager, I
asked her how to determine what opportunity to jump at.
She said, "Just keep jumping. God will open the right
one and clear a path for you." Proverbs 3:5-6 clearly tells
us to, "Trust in the Lord with all your heart and lean not
on your own understanding; in all your ways acknowledge Him, and He will make your paths straight."

Success should be measured by more than academic
achievement. A successful lifestyle is more important
than having one particular area of success. That is why
Christianity is so exciting because walking in the Spirit
gives us a successful lifestyle. God's principles are designed to truly give us success. Of course, that may not
be what the world calls success.

Success is an individualized thing. What success is for
one person may not be right for another. Even in the
day-to-day working of our Christian life we see this principle. Some evangelists reach millions while God has others only reach a handful. Both are equally obedient to
God's call. Some pastors will have gigantic churches
while others will struggle with a small congregation their
entire lives. Nevertheless, both can be equally successful
in God's plan.

Over the years, as I have presented workshops in
churches, I always ask the audience what God will say to

evangelist Billy Graham when he gets to heaven. The
workshop attenders always respond with, "Well done,
thou good and faithful servant." It's a trick question.
The answer to the question is that we have no idea what
God will say to Mr. Graham. He may say, "Bill, you blew
it! You only helped bring 20 million people into My king-
dom and I had you scheduled to reach 30 million. You
didn't accomplish My will."

On the other hand, the country pastor who faithfully
ministers to fifty people for thirty years may be doing
exactly what God intended him to do. The point is, success is personal and in relationship to God.

THE LOADED WORD

There is one word often used in connection with success
that sets a child up for failure. Unintentionally, we actually create the setting for failure by using this word. The
word is *potential*. I have spoken to thousands of people at
workshops and when I ask for a show of hands of those
who have reached their potential no one responds. It
quickly becomes apparent to everyone that no one really
knows what their potential is and to say they have
reached it would mean no more growth is possible. Yet
we often use this loaded word on our children or, as
teachers, our students.

Why do we burden a child with guilt about reaching
his or her potential when we haven't reached ours? It
reminds me of the father who scolded his son for not
doing more homework. "What do you think Abraham
Lincoln was doing at your age?" the father asked his son.
"I don't know," the son replied, "but I know what he
was doing at your age!"

Potential is a loaded word that can only highlight failure. A better word is *ability*. Ability has to do with recog-
nizable qualities that can be used to enable a person to
reach a goal. Talking about your children's abilities will
give them tangible affirmations of their skills and
aptitudes.

EAGLES AND EELS

There is a funny little story about the uniqueness of success and achievement. Once upon a time the animals decided they must organize a school. They adopted an activity curriculum consisting of running, climbing, swimming, and flying. The curriculum was standardized, requiring each animal to learn each subject.

The duck was a super swimmer, but failed miserably in running. This made him a candidate for remedial running, and he felt the sense of failure keenly when he had to stay after school for extra instruction.

The rabbit, a great runner, was put in a remedial swim class. Poor rabbit, he nearly had a nervous breakdown due to his intense fear of water. Climbing was definitely the squirrel's forte, but he couldn't fly exactly the way the instructor expected so he needed extra help. Being a diligent learner, he tried repeatedly to overcome his handicap, but the overexertion nearly killed him. Poor squirrel, he developed so many physical and psychosomatic problems that he was a candidate for the special education class for the emotionally disturbed.

The defiant eagle refused to do anything the others did. He was a terrible discipline problem and spent a good deal of time in the adjustment counselor's office learning to mend his ways. Last but not least was the eel, who, though only mediocre at everything, won the general excellence award.

Success is an individual achievement. Each person's success can only be measured by what God has granted him in ability and opportunity. Trying to make squirrels fly like eagles is never the path to true success.

BEING VERSUS DOING

Many parents say, "I only want my child to be happy." But really, what does *that* mean? You can talk to any child and family counselor and they will tell you that if you want your child to be happy, a vital ingredient is love and acceptance for just being, not doing.

Children are often most unlovable when they need love most. In the midst of their failure—when we are disappointed in them—they need our love and acceptance, not for what they did, but for who they are—God's precious gift to us.

Self-confidence and a sense of internal well-being are *learned*. As adults, we spend billions of dollars each year on motivational and success programs. One motivational speaker charges over $900 for a three-day seminar and his sessions are sold out. His videotape series for corporations sells for $12,000.

Do you know what most of these programs boil down to? Affirmation! "You're great!" "You can do it!" "Believe in yourself!" Most of these programs simply teach people how to "affirm" themselves. Children need parents to supply the affirmation. You are the ones to teach your child self-confidence and a sense of internal well-being. It will, by the way, save your child lots of money later in life because he won't need to go to one of those expensive affirmation seminars!

Dr. Cynthia Pincus, in her book *The Roots of Success*, comments that the mother's role in strongly influencing the learning direction of the child is incredible. The Japanese believe this so strongly that at the famous Suzuki system of instrument instruction, the mother learns the violin right along with the child. It is your belief in your child's ability to achieve that will be the greatest help to his or her eventual achievement.

THE IMPORTANCE OF LIFESTYLE

A successful lifestyle is more important than any one individual achievement. Pop star Whitney Houston sang for the 1984 summer Olympics, "Give me one moment in time." But one moment in time does not a life make.

While trying to get a job as a public school teacher I used to substitute teach. One day I was called to substitute for a physical education teacher at my old junior high school. I took the kids out to the baseball field to play softball for the day. While I was watching my class, another P.E. teacher who had been there when I attended the school introduced himself. As we talked he looked out over the field to where a custodian was mowing the lawn at the far end of the football field. "Do you recognize that guy?" he asked me. I indicated that I didn't. "Well, he was in your class," he reminded me. The teacher went on, "He was the big man on campus. A real athlete who won every award in the book." "That's quite an accomplishment," I said. "Yeah," my colleague replied, "but he peaked out in ninth grade. Now, he just mows our lawns for a living."

His moment in time was when he was fifteen years old! We've all met people like that who tragically had only their "one moment in time" years ago that they keep rehashing in their minds. Their self-esteem is wrapped up in an event long forgotten by everyone else. It's sad. But it happens all the time when we emphasize momentary achievement rather than lifestyle achievement. There is certainly nothing wrong with striving to achieve momentary success in something. The issue is whether or not that replaces the much greater calling of having a successful lifestyle.

A friend's story illustrates the difference between a momentary achiever and a lifestyle achiever. He was a high school football player who went on to a successful four years at a large state university. He had a powerful drive to succeed. At the age of twenty-five he set his goal in life: to be financially independent by age thirty-five.

With nothing but an old station wagon, a mop, and his dog, he began a janitorial service that looked promising. During the day he wore a suit and sold office managers on his janitorial services. Each night he put on overalls and cleaned the offices, returning the next morning in his suit to ask the customer if his "crew" did a good job.

Soon his hard work paid off and his business began to grow. By his early thirties his company had over 600 employees in two major cities. The business consumed him.

His friends knew he had "made it" when he bought a million-dollar home on a cliff overlooking the ocean. He had expensive cars and could vacation wherever he wanted (though he rarely had time to travel). But he wasn't satisfied. His job had burned him out. His marriage was increasingly strained. This he particularly could not understand because he told his wife and two children that all his hard work was only to make them happy.

Being the best in his industry wasn't enough. At age thirty-five he decided to get back into athletics and began training for the Iron Man Triathlon conducted in Hawaii. Within two weeks his training schedule consisted of swimming 3 miles a week, running 50 miles a week, and bicycling 300 miles each week. For three years he maintained world-class status in the triathlon.

But he wasn't satisfied.

Finally, after a violent outburst at an employee, he realized he was miserable and began searching for a greater meaning in life. His search led him to Jesus Christ and he trusted in Him to be his Savior. Within a matter of weeks his attitudes and priorities turned completely around. Realizing the time he had wasted, he sold his business at less than market value in order to get out quickly. He then started on the path of growing in his understanding of Christ, restoring his marriage, and reacquainting himself with his children. As he related his story to me, he concluded, "When I got to the top, I looked around and said to myself in amazement, 'Is this all there is to it?' "

The lifestyle achiever shows balance and wisdom in a wide range of life experiences. Striving for success in only one area to the detriment of major portions of his life is characteristic of the momentary achiever. General indications of the two lifestyles are as follows:

Momentary Achiever	Lifestyle Achiever
1. Extremely focused	More well-rounded

2. Chaotic personal life	Stable personal life
3. Generally self-centered	Generally others-centered
4. Needs to prove himself	Self-confident
5. Discontent	Content but not stagnant
6. Dependent on external support	Internally stable
7. Heavily influenced by trends	Long-term values
8. Humanistic viewpoint	Godly viewpoint

It may be impossible this side of heaven to have a fully developed lifestyle of achievement. We all are somewhere on the spectrum between being a momentary achiever and a lifestyle achiever. The point is to focus on well-roundedness and balance; to strive for a lifestyle of success, not just a moment.

Zig Ziglar is a dynamic, Christian motivational and success speaker. Wherever he goes throughout the world to conduct his seminars, he polls his audience regarding the qualities of successful people they admire. He comments that no matter where he is or what profession his audience is in, they identify the following qualities:

Caring	Character	Commitment	Compassionate
Dependable	Energetic	Enthusiastic	Faith
Friendly	Goal-oriented	Good listener	A finder of good
Hard worker	Honest	Imaginative	Integrity
Intelligent	Knowledgeable	Loving	Loyal
Organized	Persistent	Personable	Positive attitude
Responsible	Self-esteem	Sense of humor	Thoughtful
Wise			

If you'll notice, most of these qualities are *attitudes* rather than *skills*. They describe how a person thinks, not some training or skill he has acquired. After all, the greatest battle toward a lifestyle of success occurs in your mind, not the world around you.

Notice also that the list shows qualities of a successful *lifestyle* rather than a successful *accomplishment*. Not one luxury car or vacation home was listed as a sign of success. It didn't list becoming president of your company as a sign of success. Instead, the list reveals qualities of a way of life overall, not a singular achievement.

Most of these qualities can be *taught* and *learned*. That means your child can acquire them, use them, and *be* successful. These qualities are not exclusively reserved for a few people destined to be successful. They can be yours and your children's. They can be taught and learned.

LOCATING YOUR CHILD'S PRESENT POSITION

Before teaching your child the various qualities of a successful person, it is best to determine what qualities he or she already demonstrates. On a piece of paper list the twenty-nine qualities shown on page 51. To the right of each quality draw a line across the page and place seven dots evenly spaced starting at the left end of the line and finishing on the right end. Place the number "1" over the far left dot, the number "2" over the next dot to the right and so forth until you have numbered all seven dots. Finally, put the word "not" under number one and the word "very" under number seven.

Now, on this scale from one to seven that you have just drawn for each successful quality, plot where your child is right now. For instance, if your child is not dependable, circle number one. If your child is very dependable, circle number seven. Circle a number somewhere in between to indicate where he or she may be if not on either extreme.

This exercise is for evaluating *school-aged children*. Making character quality judgments on children under six years old is difficult if not impossible. After all, how dependable is a three-year-old? How wise is your toddler?

After evaluating your child, look for areas where he ranks low. These would, then, be things you would want to instill in your child. Apply the anchoring strategies when enhancing these character qualities in your child. Ask, "What must I teach to my child?" Develop a simple definition of, for example, dependability that you can teach him.

Second, ask, "What must I model for my child?" Brainstorm ways to demonstrate dependability to him. This could quite easily be demonstrated when you find yourself torn between something you would like to do and something you committed yourself to do. For example, you committed yourself to working on a Saturday at the church, but later a friend calls you and wants to get together that day. Here is a perfect opportunity to model dependability. Instead of simply turning down your friend's offer, let your child in on your decision-making process. In this way, he sees you demonstrate how to be dependable.

Third, ask yourself, "What can I encourage in my child?" This involves looking at those qualities for which you gave your child high marks. These are things your child is already demonstrating. Think of ways to acknowledge them and express your satisfaction with them being demonstrated in your child. Come up with ways to convey, "I believe in you" statements surrounding those demonstrated character qualities. In chapter 7 there is a three-step encouraging technique to help you do this.

SUMMARY

Having a clear definition of success is important for giving your children's lives direction. Success is living in such a way that you are using what God has given you — your intellect, abilities, and energies — to reach the purpose for which He intended your life. When helping your child develop successfully, it is best to look for identifiable abilities rather than use the loaded word *potential*. Affirmation, "I believe in you statements," are important in developing your child's self-confidence. Success is most often found in good internal character qualities that can be taught and learned by anybody. These qualities will foster a lifestyle of success which is more important than momentary achievement.

Anchoring Questions for Chapter Three:

1. What is one characteristic of a successful person you can teach your child in the next thirty days?

2. How can you model the characteristic you are teaching your child?

3. What characteristic is your child demonstrating that you can encourage?

4

Navigate Life's Reefs with God's Moral Compass

Navigating Principle #4: Successful living is based on God's moral principles and your decisions to live by those principles.

When it comes to navigating the dangerous waters of life, I am reminded of the important role the lighthouse plays in guiding ships to safe harbor. In days of old there were thieves known as "wreckers" who set up false lighthouses in order to lure ships onto the rocks where they could be plundered. Some wreckers attached lanterns to an ox and walked it along a beach near treacherous rocks. This made the captain offshore think another ship was safely passing that way. He would follow to his peril. Wise captains needed to know where the true beacons were and how to navigate the dangerous waters around them. For us to live successful lives, we must use the instruments God has given us to avoid danger and arrive safely at our destination.

Franklin D. Roosevelt once said: "To train a man in

mind and not in morals is to train a menace to society."
Your children's achievement must be measured in more
than just academics. In fact, your children may be fantastic achievers RIGHT NOW! They may be achieving
MORAL success. For the most part, your children are
great achievers when it comes to avoiding drugs and
drinking, premarital sex, and dishonesty.

The pressure on them to conform to the world's standards is incredible. Hundreds of thousands of children—
even millions of children—are failing in the area of moral
achievement. When was the last time you praised your
kids for moral success? When was the last time you said
to your child, "Hey, I know the kind of pressure and
temptations you have at school, and I just want you to
know I'm proud of your moral integrity"?

Success is more than just academic achievement. Steven Muller, president of Johns Hopkins University, as-
serted: "The failure to rally around a set of values means
that universities are turning out potentially high-skilled
barbarians."

It is interesting to note that in a study of sixty mothers
of high achievers—people who accomplished greatness in
a particular field—80 percent of the mothers claimed
that "being a good person" was what they considered the
highest priority to instill in their children. They ranked
moral character above other options such as: to be independent, to be happy, to attain a standard of excellence
or high achievement, or to be well liked. So, whether you
look at God's Word, educators, or mothers who have
raised high achievers, you get the same message: Moral
character is a vital ingredient for success.

Proverbs 11:3 says, "The integrity of the upright will
guide them, but the falseness of the treacherous will de-
stroy them" (NASB). Proverbs 20:7 speaks to the importance of fathers being role-models of moral character. It
says, "A righteous man who walks in his integrity—how
blessed are his sons after him" (NASB). Why are they
blessed? Because of the example of the parent.

HOW TO HELP YOUR CHILD MAKE GODLY DECISIONS

Young people are pressured continually by their peers, by advertisers, and by the media to make bad decisions.

Having good decision-making skills and the moral foundations to make good decisions will enable your child to be discerning in life and resist social pressures regarding such things as drugs and premarital sex. Having these skills will help your child be a good problem-solver.

Foundational to success are your life values. The basis for your life values are your spiritual values. The attainment of a goal will be meaningless if it violates your basic values.

Children learn values. Parents are their greatest source of values education. We need to realize that we demonstrate values more than we explain values and children detect if there is not harmony between what we do and what we say.

Some parents and educators maintain that they don't want to impose their moral values on their children but will wait until they can choose for themselves. How unfortunate. Those same parents will not hesitate to impose their will on the child concerning dress, diet, and schedule. Many educators are fond of the slogan, "Question Authority," yet they certainly wouldn't allow any questioning of their authority in the classroom. There are many rules the teacher imposes on the children. How much more important are moral and spiritual values?

Samuel Taylor Coleridge, the great English poet of the Romantic period, was once talking with a man who told him that he did not believe in giving children any religious instruction at all. His theory was that the child's mind should not be prejudiced in any way. At a later age, the child would be free to choose his own religious opinions.

Coleridge said nothing. After a while he asked his visitor if he would like to see his garden. The man said that he would, so Coleridge took him to the garden where only weeds were growing. The man looked at Coleridge in surprise and said, "Why, this is not a garden! There are nothing but weeds here!" Coleridge answered, "Well, you see, I did not want to infringe on the liberty of the garden in any way. I was just giving the garden a chance to express itself and choose its own production."

Developing moral character is much like growing a garden. Left to itself it will soon fall into disarray. Weeds will take over and a sense of order will degenerate into chaos. A garden requires planning, planting of seed, nurturing, and pruning before it gives back to the gardener any substantial production. This makes for an excellent metaphor for developing moral character in a child.

A REEF THAT THREATENS YOUR SHIP

Most children in public schools today are taught "decision-making" skills through a method known as values clarification. This method was developed in the late 1960s by Sidney Simons and his colleagues at the University of Massachusetts. Everyone thought, "Wonderful! Now we can clarify values for kids." Sadly, we found out that this method didn't clarify what values were good and what values were bad. Instead, it clarified that *there are no values* — there is no such thing as right and wrong.

Values clarification is based on a philosophy called situation ethics. Situation ethics means that right and wrong are decided based on the situation. Since each situation changes and is different for everyone, what is right and wrong changes with the situation and is different for everyone.

Morality has to do with right and wrong and doing the right thing. It deals with behavior based on a principle. Establishing what is the right thing in a given situation is considered the realm of ethics.

Situation ethics is based on the idea that only a given circumstance and the individual's desires determine what is the right thing to do. The moral principles he chooses can change as the situation changes.

This is very different from Christian morality which states that morality is unchanging and is the basis for establishing what is right in a given situation. Rather than our desire establishing our morality in the situation, our morality establishes our desire in the situation. For instance, a person may *want* to have sexual relations with his girlfriend because it is his desire. If he bases his decision on situation ethics, he can justify acting on his desire and will eventually act on it. If he bases his decision on Christian morality, he will restrain his desire. His passions will submit to his principles rather than his principles submitting to his passions.

Situation ethics starts from the assumption that man is basically good. It relies solely on man's reason. It is assumed that if a person is just taught to reason more logically, he will naturally make the best choice. Problems in the world, so says the theory, arise because man is not reasonable enough. Thus, values clarification emphasizes a reasoned process of determining values, rather than the outcome of that process—the actual value itself.

One moral philosopher who writes material for educators states, for instance, we must have "faith in reason" (quite an oxymoron!). Yet he gives no reasons for having such faith.

Ironically, this "reasoned" approach to determining morality falls prey most easily to emotionalism. Decisions are based on desires and desires are governed by passions. In the end the person using the values clarification methods ends up merely using reason to justify his or her emotion-based decisions.

It would be unfair to characterize this philosophy as supporting only the "If-it-feels-good-do-it" idea. The situation ethicist may do something inconvenient such as protest against something in society. But the basis for choosing the belief that leads to protest is emotional rather than rational. When asked, "Why do you think such-and-such is wrong?" that person falls back on emotional arguments.

For instance, on the issue of abortion, a pro-abortion protester, when asked why he is for abortion may respond, "Because choice is important." When asked why choice is important he may respond, "Because that is freedom." When asked why freedom is important, he may rummage around for an answer but eventually it falls back on the simple realization that it is *his* desire. His wish. His emotion.

Christian morality, on the other hand, starts with God's absolute principles. Flowing from those principles comes a logical sequence of reasoning. The individual's emotions do not determine the morality of a particular choice. Emotions play the part of the responder to principle, not the initiator of it.

Obviously, being human we are all prey to our emotions and Christians make emotional rationalizations of immoral behavior just like others do. The difference is, the Christian has a strong foundation in biblical absolutes from which to construct his ethical system. This allows him a consistent framework in which he can think logically about moral behavior. The humanist bases his decision on self-established principles which can change at any time. Though he may be "logical" within the system of his own making, his entire system can change with his desires.

When your child is taught this idea in school, most of the time he is not told outright about situation ethics and the idea that everything is relative to his emotions. Instead, he learns this when: (1) he is told that *all* options are to be considered in a situation; (2) he is told that *everyone's* idea of right and wrong is *equally* valid— it's just a matter of personal opinion and; (3) he is put in "moral dilemmas" where he is forced to choose between two wrong decisions rather than a right one.

Values clarification is based on the idea that there is no right and wrong. It stresses the process of forming a value rather than the actual value itself. It teaches seven factors in the process of defining personal values:

1. It must be *freely chosen.*
2. Chosen from alternatives.
3. Chosen after careful consideration of the consequences of each alternative.
4. Prized or cherished.
5. Publicly affirmed.
6. Acted upon.
7. Acted upon regularly.

When you look at those seven factors you realize that *we all use those things in making a decision.* For instance, think about how you chose your spouse. You went through that process. I hope you chose freely and you chose from alternatives. You carefully considered the consequences of each alternative (of course, you might feel that you weren't quite ready for some of the consequences of your choice!). You cherished your decision and publicly affirmed it and you consummated your marriage, thus affirming your decision. We all use that method to some degree.

But there are two things wrong with it. First, God is absent from that system. Alternatives are looked at but not in light of God's divine standards.

When your child is taught values clarification in school, he is taught how to make a decision without God. God doesn't enter the picture. In fact, values clarification is hostile to anyone who uses either tradition or divine authority as the basis of a decision. That, it is said, is not *freely* choosing from alternatives. Instead, values clarification uses the group process of discussion to arrive at what is right and wrong. The student is to find his own answer by hearing diverse input and developing his own ethical system.

That leads to my second concern with this method: Helping kids become good decision-makers will not necessarily help them make good decisions.

William Kilpatrick, associate professor of psychology at Boston College and an insightful Christian writer, puts it this way: "Moral development is not simply a matter of becoming more rational or acquiring decision-making skills. It has to do with vision, the way one looks at life."

Just because our schools teach children how to make decisions does not mean they are learning how to make *good* decisions. It is very easy to be careful, cautious, and thoughtful . . . and make the wrong decision. Our prisons are full of people who went through the values clarification process and got caught acting on their cherished values.

Being a moral person often means *not looking at any alternatives*. When our children are faced with the decision of whether or not to be honest, do we really want them to examine all the alternatives before deciding to be honest? Do we want them to think that being honest and being dishonest are equally valid depending on the situation? No! We want them to be honest. They will find opportunities to be dishonest quite easily on their own.

Values clarification assumes that every child is a moral philosopher—a miniature Socrates. Here's how your child is asked to be a little Socrates. Values clarification is taught through moral dilemmas. The lifeboat game is probably the most infamous example of this. Ten children are asked to sit in a circle and pretend they are on a lifeboat adrift at sea. But in order for nine to be saved, one must be thrown out of the boat. The question of who should die is then asked.

The children take on different roles such as doctors, cooks, or policemen and have thirty minutes to "plead" their case for why they are important to the group and should live. When the time is up, a vote is taken and, by mob rule, one person is "killed."

Following this morbid activity a discussion takes place to find out what values where brought out by the game. Nothing is said about the value of human life. Nothing is said about the self-esteem of the child rejected by the group. Nothing is said about the violent act of the group. Nothing is said about the stereotyping of people based on a brief description such as, "carpenter." Certainly nothing is said about God's provision and sovereign will.

Parents have reported that Christian children who are involved in these games and use the Christian value of giving up their lives for friends are given failing grades for not participating properly (even though they are truly acting on their values).

Other variations on this theme are found in the cave-in game and the fallout shelter. The cave-in game involves the children pretending to be in a cave that is collapsing. In order to get out they must form a single-file line. The person at the head of the line is most likely to survive. The question then is, "Who goes first?"

In all these exercises values are derived from the situation. Ethics are considered momentary and only based on how well they serve the individual making the decision— not on whether they are morally right. The only basis for what is morally right in this philosophy is what serves the apparent "need" of the individual or group.

The philosophy used in our public schools through values clarification conforms to the philosophy of humanism. Listen to what a society of humanists wrote as part of their Humanist Manifesto:

"We affirm that moral values derive their source from human experience. Ethics is autonomous and situational, needing no theological or ideological sanction. Ethics stems from human need and interest."

Of course the question that highlights the failure of this thinking is, "What human need and whose interest are we talking about?"

Joseph Stalin and Mao Zedong used this exact philosophy to justify the slaughter of some 50 million of their own countrymen!

The danger of values clarification being taught to children is that your child's moral assumptions can be dissolved in the climate of subjectivism, decision-making, and weighing all the alternatives that values clarifiers create in public classrooms.

If your child has developed a core set of values based
on Christian principles, those values can be eroded in a
constant climate of subjectivism. All alternatives are giv-
en equal status in the discussion. Those people who hold
to strong moral convictions and condemn those who
choose otherwise are viewed as narrow-minded, old-fash-
ioned, and backward. This puts great pressure on the
child to conform to a relativistic view of life in order to be
accepted by his or her peers. It doesn't instill convictions,
it instills ambivalence. It doesn't create decision-makers,
it promotes indecisiveness.

NEUTRALIZING THE EFFECTS OF VALUES CLARIFICATION

How do you neutralize the damaging effects of "decision-
making" courses that teach situation ethics? What can
you do as a parent? I suggest two things you can do.
(1) You can change what is happening in the classroom;
and (2) you can teach your child to stand strong against
situational ethics by teaching him or her God's moral
standards.

Winning the Teacher

Winning the teacher to your position is important. You
can change what is happening in the classroom by per-
suading the teacher of values clarification's flaws. First,
point out that it is intrinsically hostile to those who look
to *tradition* or to *divine authority* as the basis for values.
Personal freedom reigns supreme over moral authority.
Second, teaching only decision-making skills does not
necessarily enhance moral development. The *apparent*
consequences of a decision may not lead to the right decision. For example, a lie may *seem* at first to have little
negative consequences but in hindsight may inflict far-
reaching damage.

Values clarification can be neutralized in the classroom
if you can convince the teacher to also include the importance of making decisions consistent with *family* and *re-*

ligious beliefs. You can point out that not only does this provide a basis for making decisions but it also helps the teacher avoid future conflict with parents.

Teaching Godly Decision-Making

It is not enough to be able to make decisions, they must be godly decisions, decisions that are pleasing to God. Morality is concerned with what is right and wrong, but it goes beyond just understanding what is right. It also means *doing what is right.*

When you do what is wrong, that action is called immoral.

There are six elements in moral development. The approach to decision-making which follows is very different from values clarification because it is concerned with character formation rather than merely rationalization of choices.

To make it easier to remember the six key elements in moral development, I have outlined them by using the word, MORALS:

M   =   Mindful of the truth
O   =   Observe good examples
R   =   Read virtuous stories
A   =   Assume a moral core
L   =   Look at the options
S   =   Standard responses

"M" stands for "mindful of the truth." What is God's standard for right and wrong? What does He expect of us? This is radically different from situation ethics because it assumes that there is an objective truth that we can discover.

Space does not permit us to cover all of God's moral laws but it is important that your children go to church and receive instruction in righteousness from you at home.

Christianity has, from its beginning, emphasized objec-

tive truths that are eternal. It is the duty of humans to
know these truths and conform to them. However, it
may be good to also look at a secular source as well. This
may help you when talking with an educator in the public school system.

William Kilpatrick points out that, "Plato maintained
that the well-bred youth is nurtured from his earliest
days to love the Good and Beautiful 'so that when Reason at length comes to him, then bred as he has been, he
will hold out his hands in welcome and recognize her
because of the affinity he bears to her.' "

Notice that Plato recognized that reason does not lead
him to *love* the Good and Beautiful but simply to *recognize* it. Upbringing causes the child to *love* it. Plato maintained that there are objective and eternal truths that we
must discover and to which we must relate. The concept
of absolute truth *can* be taught in a secular classroom.

"O" stands for "observe good examples." Children learn by imitation, and young people are challenged
by inspiration. Are you a good example of moral character? Are you a good, moral decision-maker? Do you inspire your child to imitate people with moral character?

So much of what a child sees today emphasizes bad
behavior—even when that behavior is condemned. For
instance, the nightly news certainly does not condone
crime. Yet, crime and corruption make up the majority of
news and thus, the majority of examples to be observed.
Think of what a difference could be made by seeing news
of heroes and moral achievers.

Be sure to point out to your children people who are
doing the right thing. Help your children understand
what the moral person has done and why it is right.
Make this a habit.

"R" is for "read virtuous stories." This is a major
flaw of values clarification. The stories it uses are not
virtuous. No attempt is made to identify moral character;
no traditions, loyalties, or history come into play; and
endings are left "up in the air."

Kilpatrick comments on the importance of stories in shaping moral development: "Stories of virtue, courage, and justice can and should play a central part in the formation of good habit—that is, in the formation of character."

Bible stories are important in shaping moral character. People learn character development by *imitation* and *inspiration*. Bible stories not only give us insight into divine principles, they also show us how to live here on earth. David's courage before Goliath, Joseph's purity in Potiphar's house, or Solomon's choice of wisdom over riches are wonderful examples to us in how to live.

A mother who attended a *Charting Your Family's Course* seminar related that, one night after reading the story of Jonah and the whale before bedtime, she was talking with her three-year-old son. She told him how much she loved him and that they would be together forever. "I'm leaving when I'm sixteen years old," the child responded. "Oh? And where are you going?" the mother asked. To which the boy quickly responded, "To preach the Gospel in Nineveh." Stories can have profound impact on establishing moral and upright behavior.

"A" stands for "assume a moral core." It means certain moral standards are taken for granted. An example of someone who assumed a moral core can be found in the life of Joseph. When Potiphar's wife wanted to sleep with him, what was his response? "How can I do this sin against God?" Joseph didn't look at the range of alternatives and consider the consequences of his decision. He assumed a certain morality.

As your child becomes mindful of the truth, observes good examples, and reads virtuous stories, he or she will *assume a moral core*. Certain things are taken for granted. A person should do "this" and should not do "that."

Our minds are corrupted by sin and our sin nature is constantly looking for ways to rebel against God. By looking at all the alternatives as morally equal, we are asking what Satan did in the Garden: "Hath God said?" This is not an irrational position as many educators would like to believe. Assuming a moral core fixes limits and establishes order. For example, our legal system has enough trouble as judges try to interpret our Constitution. Can you imagine the chaos that would occur if each judge made up his own Constitution and changed it from week to week?

That is similar to teaching our children to make decisions based on their own subjective experience. Our children don't need to ponder all the exceptions to the rules; they will do that quite naturally. They need to know the rules to such an extent that they assume a moral core.

After having the foundation for moral decision-making, we must then engage in evaluation.

"L" stands for "look at the options." This involves evaluation, not necessarily consideration. It is not good to consider doing certain things. But we should evaluate all things based on the assumption of God's moral core. By looking at the options in light of God's moral standards, our children can learn to evaluate options properly. Everything is not for consideration but everything must come under biblical evaluation.

This evaluating step involves judgment and discernment. Currently, there are drug abuse programs used in public schools that emphasize just the opposite. This may come as a shock to parents and educators alike. Even the educators who teach these programs do not readily recognize this terrible flaw. The absence of judgment, however, is taught when children are told to consider all the alternatives in a situation and not be narrow-minded in condemning others. This, it is said, is the basis for a democratic society: allowing freedom of choice without condemnation. It only causes lack of discernment. What is needed most by children when faced with peer pressure and media manipulation is insightful judgment, not its absence.

"S" stands for "standard responses." Decisions

involve looking at choices and then choosing, setting your course, resolving in your heart what you will do.

Once you assume a moral core, you can have standard responses: Is premarital sex wrong? Yes. Is adultery wrong? Yes. Is honesty right even at great personal cost? Yes. Is compassion right? Yes.

Again, our children don't need to ponder the exceptions. They will do that on their own. They need to know the moral core so they will have *standard responses*— reflex reactions.

Joseph's reaction to Potiphar's wife was a standard response. David's refusal to kill Saul was a standard response, "I cannot lift a finger against my master, for he is God's anointed."

The major flaw in the current way our public schools teach moral development is that they believe that you "figure out" morality. You don't "figure out" morality, you *learn* it.

TEACHING YOUR CHILD DISCERNMENT

When nonbiblical viewpoints are addressed in the classroom, this can be a perfect opportunity to teach your child discernment. The school can be a laboratory for examining how the world deals with life. We need not run from it. We can evaluate it.

When a teacher teaches situation ethics, you can teach your child God's absolutes. When your child is taught sex education at school, you can teach the biblical view of love and marriage. When abortion is endorsed in the classroom, you can explain the value of human life. When evolution is preached in science class, you can instruct your child in creationism.

Trust your gut feeling about whether or not your child is old enough sit through some classroom sessions. For instance, if you have young children, it may be fine for them to sit through a lecture on evolution, but it may be harmful for them to read too sexually explicit material. On the other hand, don't pull your eighteen-year-old from every lecture with which you disagree. Certainly that young person is old enough to learn discernment. The fears of some parents, when trying to "protect" their older children, reveal more about their lack of instilling discernment in their children than the actual harm threatened by a particular course.

SUMMARY

Successful living is based on God's moral principles and our decisions in keeping with those principles. Moral behavior can have logical reasons behind it, but it is not simply a matter of "figuring it out." Modern education believes that your child is basically good and only needs to be taught to be more rational in order to do the right thing. Thus, education's emphasis is on the process of decision-making rather than the outcome, or moral, chosen. It is said to be morally neutral when, in reality, it promotes relativism. Your child, unfortunately, has a corrupted nature and he is in need of redemption and refinement—moral restraint. This comes through learning what is right and being encouraged to follow it. In all of this it is important to teach your child discernment and good decision-making skills based on convictions about what is right and wrong.

Anchoring Questions for Chapter Four:

1. What is one moral virtue you can teach your child in the next sixty days using the six-step godly decision-making process?

2. How can you model that particular moral virtue so your child can "observe a good example"?

3. What moral successes is your child having for which you can praise and encourage him or her right now?

5

Chart Your Family's Course with Goal-Setting

Navigating Principle #5: Self-management is the key to achieving anything.

Admiral Peary is famous for reaching the North Pole. But a little-known Norwegian named Roald Amundsen conquered the other great Arctic challenge of finding the Northwest Passage—a continuous water route across North America, which until Amundsen's adventure, was only a myth. Other ships that had sailed throughout the Arctic region had been large—200 to 400 tons. Amundsen believed a smaller ship would be better suited. He outfitted an old fishing sloop of only 50 tons for the arduous trip. He selected a crew of only seven men and packed enough food to last five years. In the summer of 1903 he set sail heading northwest from Norway. For six months he forged through rough seas, fog, and ice pack until he was forced to winter at the north end of Hudson Bay. For two years he, his ship, and seven crew members were locked in the ice. Two years!

No radio, no communication, no progress. Yet, in his
mind, Amundsen never gave up. Finally, in the summer
of 1905, the ice parted and he pressed on. Months of
hardship continued until one day he spotted another vessel in the distance. Amundsen hoisted his Norwegian
flag. The other ship responded by hoisting the American
flag. It turned out to be a Yankee whaler from San Fran-
cisco! Amundsen knew his quest was almost complete.
Yet, for six more months he was locked in the ice off the
northern coast of the Yukon. Not until the summer of
1906, three years after setting sail, did he arrive to a
hero's welcome in Nome, Alaska. Roald Amundsen had
achieved his goal against impossible odds and discovered
the Northwest Passage! His tenacious persistence and
disciplined self-management caused him to turn his
dream into a reality.

Self-management is leadership you can teach your children. It will enable them to take initiative and responsibility for the direction of their lives. The self-management process will enable your children to navigate the
waters of life by the goals they set and work to achieve.

Setting goals and achieving them is absolutely crucial
to becoming successful. Goals give your life purpose.
Children need to be encouraged to think about what they
want, and how they want to achieve it. You can do this
by simply asking your child: "What do you want to get
out of your math class?" "What do you think you'll have
to do to make the varsity team?" "How do you propose
to get the money for the new bike you want?"

Setting goals is a challenge to us all. Though we are
talking about setting goals with your children, you may
need to ask yourself what *your* goals and ambitions are.
If you feel things are not going according to plan, it may
be because there really is no plan.

God has programmed a very powerful force into your
children—the desire to achieve. It is one of the most
powerful forces within a human being. God put it there.
It is reflected in things like the instinct to survive, to

procreate, to learn, to create. These things provide for the continuation of the human race.

Your children have a natural desire to achieve but that desire may be buried under piles of past failure. If children face too much failure, they may lose confidence in their ability to achieve. Goal-setting can break them out of a cycle of failure by showing them that to get what they ultimately want, they must strategize with short-term, attainable goals.

People are generally motivated better by goals that they set themselves. Children are no different. Find out what your child's goals and ambitions are. Don't worry about your child's initial goals. As they mature, their goals will change.

The important thing is that they have a sense of ownership of a particular goal and that they begin achieving toward that goal. Long after your child's dream of being, for instance, a high-risk stuntman has faded, his self-confidence from making some initial strides in that direction will stick with him. His youthful ambition for being a high-risk stuntman can be channeled into short-term, achievable goals such as good physical fitness, coordination, courage, and safety-awareness. Later in life he will look back and chuckle at his idea of being a stuntman, but his accomplishments toward that goal will still be with him.

Every child has an unknown potential ability. But to have developed ability, a child must combine three important ingredients:

ABILITY + DESIRE + EFFORT = ACHIEVEMENT

Your child actually has tremendous ability. It may not yet be developed, but it's there. He or she also must want to achieve and must be willing to make the effort. Any real achievement comes through the willingness to make sacrifices to achieve a goal.

As one person quipped, "Even if you are on the right

track, you'll get run over if you just sit there." The *will*
to achieve provides the fuel for great accomplishment.
You can stimulate your child's will to achieve by helping
him see the relationship between what he wants and the
small accomplishments toward getting there.

GOD'S GOVERNMENT AND
MY MANAGEMENT

Setting goals is important for children. It provides them
with a sense of accomplishment, power, and control. Everyone needs to sense that they have power and control
over the direction of their life. This is not meant to exclude God's directive hand. There is nothing more exhila-
rating than living under the directive will of God. Any
goal we have must be subservient to God's general will
for our life. What I'm talking about is the day-to-day
need to feel as though what you set out to do and what
you accomplish are directly related.

A child's confidence in his ability to achieve will increase significantly when he sees that what he sets out to
do, he can accomplish. That success will breed more success. When you help your child establish goals and encourage the attainment of those goals, you are contributing to the development of your child's sense of well-
being.

A dynamic balance must occur between God's government over your life and your management of your life.
God directs our life. He gives us principles by which we
are to live and His Holy Spirit actually directs our personal affairs.

God wants you to succeed. He gave you His Spirit to
live in you and assure success. He has a plan for you and
is guiding you in that plan. However, He also holds you
accountable for making choices and commitments. He
holds you responsible for making plans and taking persistent action toward those plans. In other words, God expects you to manage your life in accordance with His will.

Under God's government you will find that He has a

plan for you, yet you must commit your way to Him. God has standards for you, but you must let His Spirit and His Word guide your decisions, commitments, and actions. He has blessings for you, but you must allow Him to produce success in your life.

If we are not responsible to manage our lives, the writers of the New Testament wasted a lot of ink. Turn to almost any page in the New Testament and you will find direct orders for Christians to manage their lives. For instance, Romans 15:1 says, "We who are strong ought to bear with the failings of the weak and not to please ourselves." Galatians 6:4-5 says, "Each one should test his own actions. Then he can take pride in himself, without comparing himself to somebody else, for each one should carry his own load." These passages, as well as hundreds more, all carry with them the assumption that you, dear Christian, must manage some aspect of your life.

Your management under God's government means that you must make commitments regarding what you will do with what God has given you and what He requires of you in all areas of life.

The glue that holds the balance between God's government and your management is rapport. A rapport with God is vital for effectively managing your life under His government.

RAPPORT WITH GOD

Deuteronomy 6:5 commands you and me to "love the Lord your God with all your heart and with all your soul and with all your strength." Rapport means a relationship marked by harmony, conformity, and affinity. To have peace with God is the height of success. To live in harmony with God's principles, to be conformed to His plan, is the *greatest* thing you or your children could possibly achieve.

David had a wonderful rapport with God. In Psalm 42:1 he writes, "As the deer pants for streams of water,

so my soul pants for you, O God." In 73:25 he writes,
"Whom have I in heaven but you? And being with you, I
desire nothing on earth."

A rapport with God will give your life purpose. From
that purpose comes an inner sense of well-being. That
inner sense gives you the confidence to achieve your
goals. But your goals will then have a much more far
reaching purpose: accomplishing the will of God.

King Solomon said it well in Ecclesiastes 12:13, "Now
all has been heard; here is the conclusion of the matter:
Fear God and keep His commandments, for this is the
whole duty of man."

Rapport with God is the basis for successful goal-
setting. Everything springs from it. It will be your children's commitment to be conformed to the image of
Christ that will give them direction, purpose, stick-to-
itiveness, and stability in facing the challenges of life.

Excite your children about the dynamics of a close
walk with God. God isn't some kind of cosmic traffic cop
with a list of rules, just waiting to catch you breaking
one. Instead, He is like the patient driving instructor
who wants to teach us to do it right in the first place.
The best way to excite your children about the Christian
way of life is to be a good role-model.

BENEFITS OF TEACHING CHILDREN TO SET GOALS

Learning to set and meet goals has tremendous benefits
in life and is one of the most important skills you can
teach your children. Goals help translate God's values
and purposes into everyday life.

The question that we should ask after every biblical
principle is, "How do I incorporate that in my life?" That
requires setting a goal and doing it—each day.

Another important benefit of goal-setting is that your
children will learn to take initiative. Goal-setting is pro-
active. It looks for what must be done to achieve success
and it actively moves toward that.

Goal-setting also teaches children to be accountable. Once a goal is set, a person's activity can be measured by whether or not the goal is met. Often people have trouble setting goals because they do not want to be held accountable. They fear failure. Setting a goal, in their minds, is simply risking another failure. If no goals are set, there is no standard to measure success or failure.

When your children learn to set and meet goals they will be learning how to succeed day-by-day. Most of television today shows people having obtained a certain degree of success but not *how* that success was achieved. Television characters suddenly have wealth. Children are not exposed, by these shows, to the daily decisions and habits that went into being successful in business. Consequently, young people grow up wanting the rewards but not really knowing the work that is required to receive them.

Successful people in any field are those who make a habit of doing the things that failures don't want to do. Persistent pursuit of goals leads to success. As someone once quipped: "Inch by inch, it's a cinch; yard by yard, it's hard; mile by mile, it's futile."

Another important lesson learned from goal-setting is how to handle obstacles and setbacks. Goals require action steps. These action steps help us overcome disappointments and delays. Often children will give up on a goal because they are only looking at the end result. The first obstacle that jumps in their path discourages them too easily.

It's similar to rock climbing. As the climber ascends the cliff, he sets small anchors in the rock and runs his lifeline through them. If he loses his grip and falls, he will only fall a few feet until the last anchor holds him secure. By having a clear set of action steps the child can simply retreat to the previous step and reassess how to overcome the new problem. Discouragement won't set in so easily because the child knows that he or she is in control rather than merely the victim of circumstance.

This brings up another important benefit of goal-setting: It helps children feel a sense of power and control in their lives. We all want control of our lives. It is natural and healthy. No one wants to be the slave of circumstances or of other people. Free will and a reasonable amount of independence is good.

A friend of mine was sailing along the Central American coast when he was captured by the Nicaraguan Sandinistas and falsely accused of being a CIA gunrunner. He was detained for about forty days. He told me later that the worst part of the terrible odyssey was the feeling of helplessness. He was told when to sleep, when to eat, when to talk, when to keep quiet, when to stand, and when to sit. He had no control over his physical life during his time in jail there. It took him several years to work through the anger he felt toward his captors just for being trapped for forty days.

You may feel that way about your life. You may be trapped because you have never set any goals. You feel powerless to do anything about your situation. Take courage. Goal-setting and some self-discipline to achieve your goals can help you break free from your feelings of despair. Imagine how much worse your children could feel. They, of all people, have little power and control in their lives. They depend on adults for almost everything. By teaching them to be goal-setters, you are giving them an important tool for gaining maturity and eventual independence.

Goal-setting also teaches children the organizational skills necessary for achievement. Certainly there are those people who stumble into success. But most successful people have some sort of plan. If I am going to be successful, for instance, in memorizing Bible verses, I must set a goal that involves organization. I must choose the verses, set aside time to work on them, have a place to write them down, and have a method for monitoring my progress. I must be organized. Achievement rarely happens by accident.

Finally, goal-setting teaches your children to be leaders. Very few people actually set goals. Those who do often rise as the leaders within a group. Goal-setting teaches the things outlined above. These are the ingredients of leadership.

The best definition of leadership I have found comes from Bobb Biehl, a Christian business consultant. He defines it as knowing what to do next, knowing why that is important, and knowing how to bring the resources together to make it happen. The person who is regularly setting and achieving goals asks the questions that determine what to do next, why it should be done, and what it will take to make it happen.

A business magazine recently published an article on the impact of clearly written goals. It pointed out a survey of Harvard business school graduates concerning their goals ten years after graduating from that prestigious school. The survey found that an astounding 83 percent of the graduates had no goals at all. Another 14 percent said they had goals but didn't have them written down. However, this group was earning three times more than the first group. Even more to the point, only 3 percent of the graduates had clearly written goals. They were earning ten times more than the group that had no goals at all!

GUIDELINES FOR GOAL-SETTING

Goal-setting is easy but it does take some time and effort. There are four simple ingredients of successful goal-setting. After reading this section, I suggest you try your hand at setting a simple goal that you can accomplish within two or three days. This will give you practice in using the principles of goal-setting. Often we get discouraged about goals because we only think of them in terms of large "wish list" items such as losing forty pounds or spending thirty minutes each day in Bible study. When we fail to reach those big goals, we conclude that we are failures at achieving goals in general. Start small and gain practice at the skill of goal-setting and goal accomplishment.

1. Any goal you set must be realistic. The goal needs to be obtainable. An ambition is bigger than a goal. Your child may have a lifelong ambition. That's fine. But he also needs obtainable goals.

Goals become unrealistic when you don't give yourself enough time to accomplish them. Be sure to set a realistic deadline. You may find it helpful to increase your initial estimate of how long it will take to accomplish the goal by 50 percent. This will guard against unexpected interruptions.

Another thing that can make goals unrealistic is when you have too many to accomplish at once. This is the classic mistake of New Year's resolutions. We try to accomplish too many goals during the month of January and by February we have given up. Choose the appropriate time frame within which you will complete the goal. It is fine to set a goal that you won't even start working on for six months. That is not procrastination, it's wise planning. Pace yourself.

For instance, Johnny and his dad sat down to look at the categories for setting specific goals. Johnny really didn't have any good friends so when it came to "Friendships," Johnny said he wanted to set a goal of making friends. At first Johnny wanted to set a goal of making eight friends. But after talking about it with his dad, he decided that making one good friend by the end of four weeks would be a good goal.

Another problem with some goal-setting is that it is not realistic because you have no desire to accomplish the stated goal. Maybe it's something you feel you should do but really don't want to do. You will have problems in being motivated to work toward the goal.

If this is a problem, reexamine your goal and see if you can come up with a better motivation for accomplishing what you know you must do. For instance, you know you have to fix the fence in your backyard but you hate the thought of doing it. You just can't stand carpentry work. Your dislike for hammer and nails has kept you from getting around to fixing the fence. Back up and look for other motivators in this task. Upon taking a second look you realize that your dog, which you love very much, has had to be tied up because the old fence wouldn't stop him from running into the street. You want your dog to enjoy the freedom of playing in the backyard. There's your motivation. Now, every time you think of the goal of fixing the fence, think of how this will benefit your dog. Create the desire for goal accomplishment.

2. Define your goals specifically. The more specific your goal, the easier it is to identify the best path toward achieving it. Your child may want to be an athlete. But in what sport? After deciding what sport, he will also need to decide what position to play.

When defining specific goals, it is important to set goals that are relevant to your child—something he or she really wants to accomplish. Remember, their ABILITY is not enough; they must also have the DESIRE and be WILLING to make the EFFORT.

A man once told me how specific goal-setting helped his daughter. She approached him one day and asked if he would buy her a bicycle. He responded by saying that that was a good goal and he would help her write out the action steps needed to earn the bicycle. She began to whimper and walked away. The next week she asked him again if he would buy her the bike she wanted and he, again, encouraged her to earn it. The third week she asked again and the father responded patiently with the same suggestion of setting up a goal and action steps for earning the bicycle. Finally, she said she was ready to earn the bike.

The first thing they did was go to the bicycle shop and choose the exact bike she wanted. It was red and had ribbons on the handlebars. Her goal became very specific. Next, she outlined various chores and small jobs she could do to earn the money and she figured it would take

her six months to accomplish it. She began working on
her plan of action. Within three months she had earned
all the money she needed and purchased the bike.

The father told me of another amazing thing he discovered through all this: After accomplishing her goal, her
grades went up. She realized that she could set a seemingly impossible goal and do it. She carried that new
empowerment into her schoolwork as well.

Without defining a goal specifically, its accomplishment is much more difficult. By making the goal as tangible as possible, you will enhance your desire to accomplish it and you will have a clearer picture in your mind
as to what you must do to achieve it.

**3. Immediately break down your specific goal
into smaller steps.** Until a goal is reduced to manage-
able objectives so you can act, it is not a goal, it is a
dream.

My parents' desire to travel to Europe is a good example of the difference between a goal and a dream. They
have, for years, talked of vacationing in Europe. My father's ethnic heritage is Swiss and my mother's is Irish.
Every year they talk of going to Europe "someday."
However, when I ask them when they will go, where they
will go, and how much money they have saved toward
their trip to the "old country," their answers are vague.
They respond that as soon as they get a break from work
(my father is self-employed), they will go. But that break
never happens. Why? Because the trip is a dream, not a
goal. The moment they set a travel date, determine the
cities they will visit, and calculate the cost, they will have
a goal.

The length of time it takes to accomplish a particular
goal should be geared for the age of your child. Young
children need very short-term goals with very tangible
payoffs. Teenagers can look farther down the road. As a
person grows older, he learns to delay gratification longer
to achieve a goal.

But all of us need to break larger goals into smaller,

more immediate goals. Success at these short-term goals gives us motivation and momentum to continue toward the larger goal. If you tried to climb, in one step, over a wall that was thirty feet high, you would find it unachievable. But you could quite easily climb on top of a wall that was only six inches high. Now, all you would need to do is stack sixty little six-inch walls in such a way that by "climbing" to the top of each one you would soon find yourself on top of the thirty-foot wall. We call those six-inch walls stairs. Each one is a step to a higher goal.

If you find yourself discouraged by a seemingly insurmountable "wall" in life, reexamine it. Find the stair-steps that will lead you over the top. Break the larger goal into small steps.

This principle is just as vital to your children as it is to you. In fact, it may be even more crucial for a child to see at an early age that he can be successful in meeting challenges by creating smaller action steps toward achievement. Success breeds success. The more small successes a child experiences, the greater confidence he or she will have in attempting the next challenge.

RESPONSIBILITY AND SELF-MANAGEMENT

Self-discipline is a key to success in anything. A child must cross a bridge from external discipline such as parents, teachers, and rules, to internal discipline which involves plans, commitments, and desires. One speaker on leadership declares: "Show me someone who has accomplished anything of any significance, and I will show you a disciplined person." A self-disciplined person is one who is internally motivated by his own plans, commitments, and desires to make certain sacrifices while diligently pursuing a goal.

Goal-setting also encourages responsibility. The person who has set goals and is working toward them is exhibiting responsibility. Being responsible means that you are accountable for a particular thing. If your child is going to be held accountable for something, then he or she is

going to have to have good self-management or, in other
words, self-discipline.

A child often becomes responsible from being called on
to be responsible. When we are expected to be responsible, we often rise to the challenge.

If you strongly encourage your child to redo sloppy
homework because you know he can do better, you are
not being a tyrant. You are calling on him to be responsible. If you let the sloppy work go by, you are confirming
to your child that inferior work is all that he is capable of
doing. When you let your child get by with something
that represents less than his ability, you are encouraging
him to underachieve!

We have all heard the little saying that responsibility
means my response to God's ability. Well, don't let your
child pull that one on you regarding his homework. Com-
pleting your child's algebra assignment is not God's responsibility. When it comes to an individual being responsible for his conduct, the little saying should go:
Responsibility is my response to my God-given ability.

In other words, your child has tremendous ability, often neglected or discouraged, but still, it is there. To be
responsible, your child needs to have the proper response
to that ability.

Gene Bedley, elementary school administrator and the
National Outstanding Educator of the Year, wrote a good
book entitled, *The Big R, Responsibility* (People-Wise
Publications, 1985). He writes that responsibility means:

> Finding a way rather than making excuses; Seeing
> the present as the best time to act; Taking responsi-
> bility for your failures; Recognizing that each right
> and freedom you enjoy also carries with it account-
> ability; Putting signs in your life to help you re-
> member what to do.

On this last point, Bedley points out that children need
reminders to themselves more than they need to be in-

formed. If adults spend thousands of dollars to learn how to remind themselves through time-management seminars and calendar books, shouldn't we help kids learn how to remind themselves also? Time-management seminars cost American businesses billions of dollars. And do you know what most of it boils down to? Write things down in an orderly fashion so you will remember.

The story goes that a wealthy industrialist of a generation ago once called a time-management consultant. The industrialist explained to the consultant that he was responsible for a multimillion-dollar corporation, thousands of employees, dozens of factories, and thousands of stockholders. Yet, he couldn't seem to get anything done. He was always busy with work, but he seemed to be spinning his wheels.

"What should I do?" he asked the time manager.

The consultant told him to simply make a "to do" list, then prioritize the list and go from there.

The industrialist pulled out his checkbook to pay the consultant for the advice but the time manager refused, stating that after three months he would accept a check for whatever amount the industrialist thought his advice was worth.

In ninety days the tycoon sent the consultant a check for $25,000 and a note explaining that that simple list kept him on track by reminding him of what he had to do. The $25,000, he explained, was a fraction of what he was able to produce because of the reminders.

HOW TO PUT SIGNS IN YOUR CHILDREN'S LIVES

1. Put a bulletin board on their door for pinning notes to.
2. Use their lists of goals and achievement steps.
3. Give them a large calendar for hanging near their desk.
4. Give them a pocket calendar for recording assignments.

5. Teach them to always "look back" when leaving a place and ask, "Am I forgetting anything?"

Responsibility without rewards leads to bitterness and frustration. Children need to receive all kinds of recognition for being responsible. The best way to help a child learn responsibility is to consult with them by helping them establish goals and having them outline the steps to achieving those goals. From those goals, have your child write himself reminders.

GOAL-SETTING STARTS AT HOME
Humans are natural goal-setters. Just to survive we must set goals. We have to eat regularly, brush our teeth, wake up in the morning, get out of bed, go to the store, call a friend, and dozens of other routine goals.

This shouldn't be overlooked. Children who need to learn to be good goal-achievers can be encouraged by the fact that they already are achieving many goals. Draw up a list of things your child does already to take care of himself, his things, and to help others. The list could include brushing his teeth, washing his hands, making his bed, picking up his toys, doing homework, setting the table, and helping with chores. To the right of the list, draw seven columns—one for each day of the week. As your child achieves each of the listed goals, place a gold star or a check in the appropriate day. Soon he will see that he is a true goal-achiever throughout the week. He will see himself as successful.

When it comes to setting new goals, there are a few key ingredients in writing up an effective goal worksheet. At first, it may seem that spending time writing a specific plan of action for accomplishing a goal is too cumbersome. Ironically, the opposite is true. Having a clearly written goal along with achievable action steps is liberating. Your priorities become clearer. Your energy is more focused. You will become more efficient and will find yourself with plenty of extra time for spontaneous activity.

There are six simple steps in efficient goal-writing. First, use one sentence to write your goal. Your goal should be quantifiable and have a deadline. For instance, don't write, "I will read more in the future." Instead, indicate how much you will read and by when you will complete your reading: "I will read three books by December 31." Also, be sure to mark the date when you write the goal.

The second step is to list the benefits of achieving the goal. This is important for encouraging yourself when you face setbacks and obstacles. Third, list the resources you will need to achieve your goal. This step helps in determining what additional action steps may need to be taken. If you need a particular resource that you don't have, you will need to include getting it as one of your action steps.

The fourth step is listing the potential obstacles to achieving your goal. This is important for anticipating, and possibly avoiding, things that will stop you from achieving your goal. Having plan "B" ready will help you sidestep an obstacle and keep progressing toward goal achievement.

The fifth step is writing your action steps. Action steps are goals too. They are merely shorter goals. They can be accomplished more easily. If your large goal is extremely big, your action steps may need to be broken down into small steps.

Finally, the sixth step is to formulate a specific prayer regarding the goal. This is placed last not because it is least important but because, after having thought through the other steps, you will have a better idea exactly how to pray about your goal. I have assumed that the goal itself was developed after prayerful consideration of God's will for your life. Actually write out a one- or two-sentence prayer concerning your goal and pray that prayer every day. God has promised us that our prayers accomplish great things. James 5:16 tells us, "The prayer of a righteous man is powerful and effective."

SUMMARY

Self-management is the key to achieving anything. God *governs* your life, but He expects you to *manage* your life. This involves goal-setting. When setting goals, be sure to make them realistic, define them specifically, and break them into small action steps. While learning to set and achieve goals, your child will move from external to internal discipline. He will learn responsibility. God has placed within us the desire to set and accomplish goals. Teach your child simple methods for goal accomplishment and you will give him a strong tool for success spiritually and academically.

Anchoring Questions for Chapter Five:

1. What will you teach your child about goal-setting in the next thirty days?

2. How will you model what you teach?

3. What goal-setting habit is your child demonstrating that you can encourage and how will you encourage him?

6

Voyage Full Speed Ahead with Your Family

━━━━━━━━━━━━━━━━━━━━━━━━━━━━▶

Navigating Principle #6: Plotting your family's course in the ten major areas of life is essential for weathering storms and keeping on course through life's voyage.

━━━━━━━━━━━━━━━━━━━━━━━━━━━━▶

Probably nothing better illustrates voyaging into the unknown of life than the early ocean explorers. Most famous among these daring men stood Captain James Cook. During his explorations from 1768 to 1780 he logged many miles. His second voyage alone took in more than 60,000 miles crisscrossing the Pacific Ocean. The danger, thrill, and mystery of reaching an unknown destination anticipated in the distant future made careful plotting and navigating by Captain Cook all the more important. This is similar to your journey through life. Even though the future is largely unknown, having a specific direction is essential.

There are thousands of destinations you can launch toward on the sea. If you are not sure whether you should head for England or Japan, every look at the chart is traumatic. However, once you decide on England, many plotting decisions are automatically made for you. There are only a few routes to your destination. Your energies can be focused on staying on the determined course. Similarly, once you decide on what you would like to accomplish in five years or one year or even one month, your priorities become clearer.

There are ten major areas of life for which you are responsible. There may be a few more, but if you can do well in these ten, you will be doing well in life. These are not new areas. You are already doing things in each one. The issue is how well you are doing in each area. Setting goals in each of these ten areas is not burdensome, it is liberating. Just as plotting a specific course while sailing gives you an efficient route to your destination, so well-written goals in each of these areas will mean hours of extra time left over. With clear objectives in mind, you will accomplish success quicker and be able to move forward faster. Rather than have that project that you dislike face you every day, you can get it over with and devote your time to the goal you really enjoy.

The ten major areas of life are:
1. Spiritual
   2. Character building
      3. Home life
         4. Citizenship
            5. Self-education
               6. School
                  7. Finances
                     8. Avocation
                        9. Recreation
                           10. Vocation

You are already doing something in these areas. These are not new to you. But clearly written goals will mean you can have a greater degree of success and fulfillment in each area. You can then teach your children how to be successful in each area as well. Your example will do more than anything in teaching your children how to be successful "course plotters."

Before you get started on each area, it is important to remember two things. *First, setting goals in all ten areas at once may not be a good idea.* Instead, choose one goal this month that you can accomplish in twelve months. For instance, you may want to go to Hawaii one year from now. Between now and then you will need to have several action steps such as: save money, make travel arrangements, plan on what you will see, and book hotel reservations. Next month choose a second goal and again, plot how you will achieve it within twelve months. For instance, next month you may choose to establish a goal to become more politically involved in your community. Your action steps may include attending town council meetings, visiting your state legislator's office, learning about your county government, and reading the newspaper regularly. Continue this until, after ten months, you have ten goals set. On the other hand, you may be able to sit down one Saturday over a cup of coffee and establish a goal for each area all at once. I still think it is a good idea to stagger when you will start toward accomplishing each goal.

This leads to the second important thing to remember. *Avoid trying to accomplish all ten goals at once.* Spread them out over one year, two years, or even five years. Some goals you will want to achieve quickly. Other goals may take several years (of course, you will be breaking those goals into achievable action steps that can be accomplished quicker).

Read through each of the ten sections in this chapter and decide on a goal for yourself and one for your family. By setting a goal for yourself, you will not only grow in that area, but you will also be modeling goal achievement for your family. Setting a goal for your family involves teaching and encouraging.

CHARTING YOUR COURSE FOR SPIRITUAL GROWTH

Below are listed several ideas to help you start thinking about what kinds of goals to set for spiritual growth.

Read through the list and on a separate piece of paper
write down a few goals you want to set. Do not feel re-
stricted to the things listed below. These are merely of-
fered to help get you started.
- Attend church together as a family.
- Get involved in church activities.
- Start a family Bible study.
- Begin daily devotions.
- Pray together as a family.
- Pray with your spouse each day.
- Read a good book on a specific area of growth.
- Memorize Scripture.

Those are some things you can do. But it is more important to start by determining where you want to be
spiritually. Often, when we think of setting goals in our
Christian walk, we think of things like spending more
time in morning Bible reading. But Bible reading is only
a means to an end. What we must do to truly grow spiritually is ask ourselves, "Specifically where is my life lacking and how do I want to be?" Then ask yourself what
you will do to achieve greater spiritual maturity in that
area.

For instance, I recently looked at my life and determined that I was deficient in the area of giving. Being a
cheerful giver of my income to the Lord was not easy for
me. I was not consistent in my giving and frankly, I
didn't give that much. I set a goal to increase my giving
to 10 percent of my income and feel good about it. The
means to the goal was multifaceted. I had long discussions with a friend who is a generous giver and gained
his insight into the blessings of giving. I submitted to my
wife's gentle teaching on giving. She has a generous
heart and her example proved to be a wonderful role
model for me to imitate. I began focusing my Bible reading on God's provision and His greatness. By learning
more about how wonderful the Lord is, I was redirecting
my focus from the temporal to the eternal. Last but not
least, I began giving. I focused my attention on the peo-

ple and ministries we were helping through our gifts rather than on how much we were giving. Slowly my attitude began to change. I began accomplishing my goal.

Setting a spiritual goal means looking at the spiritual qualities you want to improve. The path to growth will involve a variety of things to do, but avoid making the means an end in itself. Bible reading is wonderful and much can be gained by simply doing it each day. But if you have specific spiritual growth in mind while you are reading, the Word comes alive in a new way. It pierces your heart and you will be more receptive to it.

Attending church regularly really is only an action step toward the greater goal of specific spiritual growth. The great challenge is to take an inventory of your life and be honest about areas in which you need to grow spiritually. This will give you the basis to set meaningful goals.

CHARTING YOUR COURSE IN BUILDING CHARACTER

President James Madison, often referred to as the Father of Our Constitution, stated: "We have staked the whole future of American civilization, not upon the power of government, far from it. We have staked the future of all political institutions upon the capacity of mankind for self-government: upon the capacity of each and all of us to govern ourselves, to sustain ourselves according to the Ten Commandments of God."

Character is an important element of human relationships. Character is the combination of emotional, intellectual, and moral qualities that exhibit integrity and strength before God and man. It is crucial that children learn to be people of character.

Here are some ideas to stimulate thinking about how you can enhance your own character and that of your children:

- Read (to yourself and aloud to your children) stories of virtuous people who demonstrate strong character in their lives.

• Make a habit of relating God's Word to daily decisions.
• Study the lives of people in the Bible.
• Make a list of important character traits and how to develop them.
• Teach your children decision-making skills.
• Teach your children discernment in dealing with worldly values.
• Develop a way to recognize and reward good character in your children.

Write down a goal for yourself (as a role model) and one you want to teach and encourage in your family.

CHARTING YOUR COURSE FOR THE HOME ENVIRONMENT

Creating the proper home environment for success is crucial. If there is fighting and tension at home, success in any area will be more difficult to achieve. Everything from creature comforts to food and emotional nourishment are important to being successful in life. Certainly there are those who have been successful when the home environment was not good. But this is more the exception than the rule.

Here are some goals you may want to set or that may start you thinking about other goals more appropriate for your family:
• Make family togetherness a top priority.
• Plan a family activity each week.
• Limit television viewing.
• Plan a major vacation.
• Begin a sport together.
• Begin a weekly family night together.
• Provide a good study environment for your children.
• Provide nutritional meals for the family.
• Develop better communication.
• Eat dinner together each night.

You can involve the whole family in setting these goals. Create a list of as many goals as you can. Sit down with your family and have everyone prioritize the goals according to his or her own preference. Then decide together what you will do as a family over the next year. This activity alone will create a fun way to communicate.

CHARTING YOUR COURSE
FOR CITIZENSHIP

We often give lip service to the importance of freedom and our democratic republic. But we do little to train our children in how our system of democracy works and our responsibilities to people in our community.

The dictionary defines a citizen as a person owing loyalty to and entitled by birth or naturalization to the protection of a particular state. Children need to understand that they are citizens of their town, state, and country. Each governmental body allows certain rights and protection. Understanding how those governments operate and how a citizen relates to them is important. It is also important to understand the responsibilities we have to other citizens in our neighborhood, town, state, and country.

Citizenship education is becoming increasingly important. Many children take for granted our form of government. Yet, our system is barely 200 years old and is an amazing experiment in the history of the world. Whether or not the freedoms we have continue will be up to the vigilance of each generation.

There are those in education today who use a confusing definition of citizenship to teach that we are citizens of the world. In fact, we are inhabitants of the world, but not its citizens. The world has no government to which we are to be loyal. The world has no law by which we are to abide, nor any constitution to grant us rights and privileges. Without a clear understanding of American citizenship, children lose a sense of the unique characteristic of being a United States citizen.

Here are some goals you may want to set for yourself and your family. Try to think of several others.

- Learn who your congressman, state representatives, and local officials are.
- Attend local governmental sessions such as city council meetings or school board meetings.
- Visit the state capital.
- Visit the mayor's office.
- Regularly discuss politics and voting issues.
- Teach your children how the ballot process works.
- Volunteer to help a candidate get elected.
- Emphasize compassion to those less fortunate in your community.
- Volunteer at a homeless project or other organization for those in need.
- Host a party for the families in your own neighborhood and simply get better acquainted.
- Read a book about our American Christian heritage.

Citizenship education begins at home and is taught best by example. Local events and state and national elections provide wonderful opportunities to teach children how to be a good citizen.

CHARTING YOUR COURSE FOR SELF-EDUCATION

Self-education is an important, yet often overlooked, form of education. It involves taking initiative for learning based on God-given interests, talents, abilities, and motivations to serve Him. You or your children do not know when God may choose to use you to alter history in someone else's life. He has given you unique qualities that He wants to use. Self-education develops those qualities.

Here are some ideas for helping your children pursue self-education.

- Pursue personal interests such as computers, music, art, sports, teaching, science, or travel.
- Visit a variety of businesses; attend museums; plan vacations that give opportunities for coming into contact with people, ideas, and places that encourage personal enrichment.

- Read books on a variety of interesting subjects.
- Take your children to hear lectures from people who are outstanding in their area of expertise.
- List things about which you or your children want to gain new knowledge and skills.

Remember to set a goal or two for yourself and act as a good role model for your children. Your children will judge how important self-education is by whether or not they see you pursuing it.

CHARTING YOUR COURSE FOR ACADEMIC SUCCESS

The education of children, according to the Bible, is a parental responsibility. The school should be there to assist you with this task, not take it from you. God outlined the importance of teaching children His commands. In Deuteronomy 6:6-7 it is written:

> These commandments that I give you today are to be upon your hearts. Impress them on your children. Talk about them when you sit at home and when you walk along the road, when you lie down and when you get up.

This forms a pattern for teaching a young person anything. First, it is the parent's responsibility to teach the child. God didn't say, "Send your children to someone else to learn this." Second, it is a lifestyle of teaching and learning. Gaining insight into the law of the Lord or any other subject begins at home and is an all-encompassing process.

In today's more complex educational environment we have delegated certain parts of a child's education to others who are more skilled in a specific area. The science teacher may have more information about chemistry, physics, or biology than you. So you delegate that learning to him. However, public school biology teachers today will teach your child evolution as if it were fact. This is not good science and must be corrected at home. So even in a technical area such as science, you cannot blindly entrust your child's education to someone else.

Here are some ideas to stimulate thinking about goals to set in charting your course for academic success.

- Review your child's homework daily.
- Set aside a regular time to do homework.
- Set up a television viewing calendar and restrict open access to the TV.
- Set daily, weekly, and long-term goals for school-work.
- As a parent, build a friendly relationship with your child's teacher.
- Regularly find out what is being taught to your child.
- Volunteer to be active in school projects, events, and classrooms.
- Regularly discuss with your child what he or she is learning.

CHARTING YOUR COURSE IN FINANCES

One of the biggest problems in America today is a family's inability to successfully handle its finances. Many families live above what they can afford and are drowning in a sea of debt. It is vital that young people learn how to be financially responsible. It may include being honest about your financial situation and mistakes you have made.

Here are some ideas for goals you can set for yourself and for your family.

- Help your children find ways to earn money.
- Help your children set up a savings account.
- Teach your children how money works in society. This includes concepts such as debt, loan, lend, interest, purchase, check, credit, capital, investment, savings, stocks, bonds, taxes, and insurance.
- Develop good buying habits.
- Involve your children in some of the budgeting.

- Teach your children generosity.
- Teach the habit of regularly giving to your church.

The last two suggested goals, generosity and giving, are crucial to proper money management. A millionaire who gives well over 40 percent of his income to church and charity once revealed to me an important insight. He explained that generosity is the only thing that will break the bondage of money in your life. Giving money away is like saying to that dollar, "I don't need you. You have no power over me. In fact, I get more pleasure in giving you away than I do in keeping you." That's true financial freedom!

CHARTING YOUR COURSE IN AN AVOCATION

An avocation is more than just a hobby. It is an area in which you have talents, aptitudes, and interests that can be used in God's service, community benefit, or possibly a vocation. Developing your avocation is important because you never know how God would like to use you. Here are some ideas:

- Find out what natural talents and interests your child has.
- Involve your child in home and community activities.
- Encourage your child in a variety of things such as sports, music, crafts, hunting, and camping.
- Enroll your child in specialized courses to learn skills in such areas as music, photography, ballet, tennis, or computers.

Well-roundedness is an important ingredient for having a lifestyle of achievement. Encourage in yourself and in your children the love of a variety of things.

CHARTING YOUR COURSE FOR RECREATION

Healthy living, physical fitness, and leisure time are important to a well-balanced life. If your body has too much fat or your muscles are out of shape, it will be harder to be active in pursuing your goals. You will have less energy. This is not to say you must become obsessed with fitness as have some people. The key factor is whether or not your health is hindering you from achievement in life. Your lack of exercise and proper nutrition may cause you to be tired. Energy and a zest for living are vital for the successful accomplishment of goals.

Here are some things you can do with your family to make recreation a well-balanced part of your family.

- As a family go swimming, jogging, hiking, or bicycling.
- Play outdoor games or sports.
- Develop a fitness plan for each member of the family.
- Start a healthy nutritional plan.
- Maintain personal hygiene.
- Provide breakfast each morning for your children.

CHARTING YOUR COURSE FOR VOCATION

God has a plan for your life. A vocation is the work you do (employment, trade, career, or homemaker) to fulfill God's call for providing for yourself and your family. Your children are in a period of preparation for a vocation of some sort.

Here are some ideas for helping your children decide on a vocation and prepare for it. Remember to try to list other goals that you think of on your own.

- To learn that God has a plan for each one of us.
- To discover your individuality regarding skills and talents.
- To become acquainted with a variety of vocational opportunities.
- To visit with people who work in a chosen field including mothers who are full-time homemakers.

After looking at these ten major areas of life, you may feel overwhelmed to think of setting goals in each area. Keep in mind, however, that you *already* function in these areas. The question is not about starting to do something in each area. Instead, the question is about how well you will do it. Setting goals in these areas should not be looked on as a burden but as a liberating activity.

SUMMARY

Plotting your family's course in the ten major areas of life is essential to weathering storms and keeping on course through life's voyage. Goal-setting in the major areas of life is a liberating activity. It allows you to rise above the distractions of everyday living and move confidently toward a fulfilling life.

You don't need to set all your goals at once. Try setting a new goal each month that will last for one year. After ten months you will have covered all ten areas. Remember to apply the principles of good goal-setting: Be realistic, be specific, and create smaller action steps. As you begin to do this, you will find your family voyaging full speed ahead on the ocean of life.

Anchoring Questions for Chapter Six:

1. What is one of the ten areas in which you can teach your child to set a goal in the next thirty days?

2. How can you model goal-setting in that area in the next thirty days?

3. In what area has your child set a goal that you can encourage?

Discover Buried Treasure
in Your Child

➤—————————————————————————————➤

Navigating Principle #7: Your child has many hidden treasures that, once uncovered, polished, and held up to the light of encouragement, will lead him to success.

➤—————————————————————————————➤

Pedro Do Bustamente looked intently at the note written by his dying father: "The money is there. Seek for it. I command you in the name of the Holy Virgin to give Christian burial to the bones of your sister. I pray..." The handwriting trailed off into the undecipherable scratches of a dying man.

Pedro turned his attention to another letter—one his father, Bruno, had received just one hour before his death. The letter was addressed to his father from an English sea captain. The captain explained that while sailing the whaling ship *Sadie Wilmot,* he and his crew came on a lifeboat containing the bodies of five men dead from starvation and thirst. In a tin box aboard the small craft was a note addressed to Bruno Do Bustamente. It read:

"Wrecked on an uninhabited island in lat. 7° 29' N.

long. 160° 42' E. Six of the crew drowned, also owner's child, Enracia Bustamente, and her nurse. The body of the former was buried at a spot above high-water mark, about 300 yards from a large round knob of rock, covered with vines on the eastern point bearing E. by N. from the grave. No provisions were saved except some jerked beef, packed in hide bags. Were four months on the island. Left July 3rd, 1862, in open boat, to try and reach Manila."

Pedro drew a deep breath of amazement. This note was written from the now dead captain of his father's ship, the *Bueno Esperanza,* which was transporting his father's fortune of $154,000 worth of gold and silver from Panama to Manila. Pedro realized in an instant what his father meant when he wrote, "The money is there." The bags made of hide did not contain jerked beef, but gold and silver coins!

Immediately Pedro commissioned a ship to take him to the desolate island described in the cryptic note. After several weeks of sailing, "Land, ho!" was sounded as the island came into view. Pedro and three trusted crewmen went ashore in search of his sister's grave and the buried treasure. Just fifty feet from the weathered wreckage of the *Bueno Esperanza* they found the humble grave of the little Spanish girl. Quickly they set about uncovering the sturdy coffin built from wood of the stranded ship. Pedro's sister would have a proper burial in Spain, he vowed to himself. From the gravesite the four men proceeded to the large rock mentioned in the dead seaman's note. They diligently searched around the giant boulder, but could find no evidence of buried treasure. Finally, Pedro looked up toward the top of the vine-covered rock. He began climbing it until he reached the top. To his surprise he found the boulder had a large depression in the center, over which the creepers had grown and formed a thick network. Standing in the center they could see space between the vines and the rock below their feet. The men used swords to slash the vines away.

Only dead leaves, dirt, and decaying vegetation filled the cavity. Pedro jumped down and sank up to his knees in the muck. With both hands he reached deep into the putrid mulch until his chin nearly touched it. Suddenly he felt the smooth texture of leather. He gripped it and pulled. Up came a hide bag bursting with Spanish gold coins!

FINDING GOLD IN YOUR CHILD

Just as Pedro searched diligently for his father's gold, so we must work hard to uncover our children's hidden treasures.

Two of the basic sources of motivation in a child's life are the need to achieve and the need for affirmation. One educational consultant has observed that without positive reinforcement, there is a real danger that the struggling child may conclude that he is incapable of success and unworthy of appreciation.

If you want to motivate your children toward greater achievement, let them know they are on the right track—that they have the *ability* to achieve. Your encouragement will empower your children. Each child has treasure buried deep inside him. Your encouragement is the key to uncovering it.

Many children learn to accept low achievement because they lack evidence in their lives that they *can* achieve. Failure breeds failure. Underachieving children have lots of failures. So you have to help them break out of that cycle of failure.

The art of encouragement is one way to help them gain confidence in themselves and break out of that cycle of failure. Success feeds success! One successful learning experience primes us for the next one because we expect success the next time we try something new. Your child may need to start with very small goals and small successes. But eventually those grow and each time he sets a new goal he has greater confidence that he will succeed.

A study was done of 120 superstars to see what caused

them to achieve. They all had one important common denominator: parental encouragement. The parents often sat with them during practice. They cheered them when they won and comforted them when they lost. If a child tried harder or did better than the last time, that too was a victory. Victories, victories, victories! You must find things to cheer about in your kids!

Encouragement is an art. One definition of *art* is "a specific skill which requires the use of intuitive faculties that cannot be learned solely by study." Though there are specific methods of encouragement, their application is more of an art than a science. It requires your good sense, judgment, and timing.

The famous business pioneer of the early twentieth century, Charles Schwab, once said:

> I have yet to find the man—however exalted his station—who did not do better work and put forth greater effort under a spirit of approval than under a spirit of criticism.

The art of encouragement means encouraging through affirmation. Affirmation is reinforcing a good quality in your children. Affirmation gives your children the "tools" they need to cope with difficult times.

Your children's self-image is how they perceive themselves. And when you are reinforcing their good qualities they will see that their self-image is based on *who they are* rather than *how well they perform*. You are your children's mirror. They will see themselves according to the feedback you give them about themselves.

For instance, let's say your child is running in a long foot race but he doesn't do very well. In one sense he failed, but think of the qualities you can affirm in that little runner: he has endurance; he is a good sport; he is not a quitter. Whether he won or lost he has those qualities. They will serve him well, long after that one race is forgotten.

THE DIFFERENCE BETWEEN PRAISE AND ENCOURAGEMENT

Praise and encouragement are not synonymous. Both have their place, both are good, but they are different. Praise focuses on performance. Encouragement focuses on effort or improvement. Praise takes place when achievement takes place. Encouragement is wrapped up in who the child *is* and *can be* rather than what he or she *does*.

This is especially important when dealing with an underachieving child, because most times there is not a whole lot to praise. But there are many opportunities for encouragement. Praise focuses on a child's particular and specific successes. Encouragement focuses on internal qualities that a child possesses.

Praise only comes when the final bell is rung. Encouragement can take place anywhere along the path to achievement. To remember the difference between praise and encouragement, simply remember this: Praise focuses on the right performance; encouragement focuses on good internal qualities which lead to achievement.

To encourage someone is to instill courage. Courage is a state of mind enabling someone to face danger or hardship with confidence and resolution. Courage is an important ingredient for success in any area of life. It is something the individual must have on his own, but it can be given a foundation through the encouragement of someone else.

Encouragement builds feelings of adequacy. Notice how the following statements convey that the person has the ability to do something: "I like the way you handled that," "I know you can do it," "You are improving."

HOW TO FIND YOUR CHILD'S SUCCESSES

We all strive for significance. Just like adults, young children crave acknowledgment and affirmation from the people they love most. They are driven to make those people proud of them. What they don't need is constant reminders of their own smallness. They are well aware of that.

A reporter once asked Andrew Carnegie why he hired forty-three millionaires to work for him. Carnegie explained that those men had *not* been millionaires when he hired them.

The reporter then asked, "How did you develop these men to become so valuable to you that you have paid them so much money?"

Carnegie replied that men are developed the same way gold is mined. When gold is mined, several tons of dirt must be moved to get an ounce of gold; but you don't go into the mine looking for dirt—you go in looking for gold! Start today to look for gold in your child.

Affirmation of good internal qualities creates new "comfort zones" for a child. He or she needs to feel comfortable performing at higher levels of confidence and achievement. That is one form of growth.

We all have comfort zones—areas in which we feel in control. Underachievers need these too. For instance, if a child is misbehaving in class, it may be because that is one area in which he has a degree of control. He may feel out of control academically, socially, or athletically—he cannot achieve as he would like. But when he cuts up, he is controlling the situation for the moment. Even if the price he must pay is negative attention, he still is within his comfort zone.

One strategy would be to affirm good behavior rather than scold bad behavior. Catch the child being good, rather than being bad. For example, one educational consultant suggests dealing with misbehaving children by openly acknowledging their good behavior by putting masking tape on their desk at school. Each time they do something right, put a large "check" on the tape. Be sure to do that many times every hour. Each day they can take the tape home to show their parents. This is a form of affirmation. It is conveying to the child in a tangible way that he has the ability to do well.

Affirmation of ability is so important, the famous
Suzuki method of violin instruction teaches two-, three-,
and four-year-olds how to take a bow in front of an audience as one of their first lessons. Why? Because they
know that when a little child bows, most adults will automatically applaud. The instructors say, "Applause is the
best motivator we've found to make children feel good
about performing and about themselves."

Your child already has many successes. Success, that
is, in good inner qualities. Oftentimes, though, in looking
for the gold we focus on the dirt.

The following is a list of good qualities your child has
to varying degrees. To find out which ones your child has
recently exhibited, use a piece of paper to write out five
things your child did with which you were pleased. Then,
from the list, identify one quality behind the deed.

You will notice that several qualities can be attached to
the same behavior. This is where encouragement becomes an art. It is up to you to determine what quality
you want to affirm. If your child cleaned the kitchen, was
he or she obedient, caring, neat, a hard worker, or ener-
getic? The same act could demonstrate all of those traits.
Focus on the one you want to build up in your child at
that time.

Caring	Character	Commitment	Compassionate
Dependable	Energetic	Enthusiastic	Possesses faith
Friendly	Goal-oriented	Good listener	Encourager
Hard worker	Honest	Imaginative	Intelligent
Knowledgeable	Loving	Loyal	Organized
Neat	Persistent	Personable	Positive
Responsible	Humorous	Thoughtful	Wise
Obedient	Artistic	Mechanical	Generous
Confident	Conscientious	Courageous	Fair
Understanding	Resilient	Gentle	Optimistic

Examples:
Deed: Cleaned the kitchen without being told.

Quality: Responsible
Deed: Studied hard for an assignment.
Quality: Goal-oriented
Deed: Good second effort during the game.
Quality: Resilient

A THREE-STEP ENCOURAGING TECHNIQUE

To be a good encourager you must properly convey encouraging comments to someone. Have you ever noticed how some people, especially men, encourage or compliment one another through put-downs? At the softball game, for instance, after the outfielder makes a good catch, the second baseman shouts, "Hey you bald-headed, old buzzard! Great catch . . . for an old man!" Somewhere buried deep inside the friendly insults is a compliment. It may make for a good laugh, but not an encouraging affirmation. It is so easy to neutralize an affirmation with a negative comment that conveys the thought: "You surprised me. I didn't think you could do it (and you probably won't repeat it)."

There are three simple steps to effectively convey encouragement and affirmation to someone. First, identify what behavior was done. This lets the other person know that you recognize what he or she did. It avoids "behavior roulette" brought on by comments like, "You're such a good girl." The child is left to figure out what she did within the last few days to deserve that comment. By identifying the specific behavior, she knows that you know what she did correctly.

Second, comment on the character quality the behavior reflects. You don't have to do this immediately after the child did the correct thing. If you need help in identifying a character quality, refer to the list earlier and then comment to the child. The encouraging word will have its full impact even at a time after the proper behavior was done. Remember, you are focusing more on who the person is rather than on what he or she did. But both praise and encouragement will be conveyed.

Be specific in your encouragement. For instance, rather than just saying, "You did a good job in the yard work." Also add, "You really got every leaf picked up. Your thoroughness is great!" Notice that "thoroughness" was the quality focused on. As that child begins to see himself as a thorough person, he will strive to be thorough in other areas of his life as well. The more specific you can get, the better. If you say, "You're improving," focus on a particular improvement that emphasizes a good internal quality: "You're improving! You really have a good eye for detail."

Third, make a positive statement about the person's future. Convey to your child that he not only has the character quality, but indicate to him how that will serve him in the future. This would be conveyed in comments like: "With diligence like that, in the future you will be able to . . ." or, "With intelligence like you have, you'll be able to . . ."

The three steps are simple. They deal with the past, the present, and the future. They comment on what a person did, what he has, and what he can be. It may take you a few attempts to make the three steps sound natural. Start by reflecting on your child's behaviors every few days and matching character qualities with behaviors. Then, when you are not rushed, employ the three-step encouraging technique. Eventually, the three steps will become more natural and being an encourager will become a part of your normal interaction with others.

POWER TO CONTROL EVENTS

One educational achievement specialist points out that children must ultimately appreciate that they have the power to influence events in their lives. He goes on to say that a parent who does everything for a child teaches that child to be powerless.

In fact, one survey of mothers who raised super achievers in sports, entertainment, business, and science commented that they never did anything for their children that their children could do for themselves.

That is a great point. But I want to go back to what was said about children needing to appreciate that they have power to influence events in their lives. Just from a human standpoint, that is very important for children to learn. But, as Christians, that has an entirely new dimension.

Not only can we see that our attitudes and actions affect events in our lives, but we also recognize that God influences events in our lives. That recognition is no small thing. Encouragement means instilling confidence in our inward qualities, and Christ is in us. That means that Christian encouragement is instilling confidence in Christ. *Courage* has the same root as the French word, *cour,* meaning "heart." The Bible refers, metaphorically, to the heart as the innermost part of our being. Christ and His words are at the innermost part of our being.

Ephesians 3:16-17 says, "I pray that out of His glorious riches He may strengthen you with power through His Spirit in your inner being, so that Christ may dwell in your hearts through faith." And verse 20 states, "Now to Him who is able to do immeasurably more than all we ask or imagine, according to His power that is at work within us." Colossians 3:16 also states, "Let the word of Christ dwell in you richly."

So, the Christian has a double advantage: (1) As just a human being we recognize that in many ways, we can cause our own effects. We can choose to fail. We can choose to have a bad attitude. We can choose to focus on achievement, success, and the positive. (2) As a Christian we recognize that God directs our life—that He influences the direction and outcome of our life. We can be instilled with confidence in our new inward quality—"Christ in [us], the hope of glory" (Col. 1:27).

What does that really mean for you and me? It means that whether we win or lose, whether we succeed or fail, we can have peace and an inward sense of well-being because of our confidence in Christ.

SUMMARY

Your children have many hidden treasures that will lead them to success. Uncover them, polish them, hold them up to the light—their success depends on it. Every child has wonderful inner qualities that can be encouraged. Becoming an encourager takes work. You must be determined to look for the "gold" buried under what seems like mountains of dirt. A simple way to do this is to find something your child did with which you were pleased and go beyond praising the action and encourage the inner quality that was demonstrated. This takes practice. At first you may need to write down the behavior and the corresponding inner quality. Eventually, being an encourager will come more easily. It is also important to encourage your child by instilling confidence in the indwelling Spirit of Christ and the power of His Word.

Anchoring Questions for Chapter Seven:

1. What will you teach your child about how to be an encourager to others?

2. How will you model being an encourager for your child?

3. What inward qualities is your child exhibiting right now that you can encourage?

Empower Your Child through Expectations

Navigating Principle #8: The most powerful force in human relationships is expectations.

Think about it. You pattern your life around expectations. You conform to expectations from God, from your church, from your spouse, your family, your children, your employer, your country, your friends, and yourself.

You are expected to live a certain way, to believe a certain way, to think a certain way, to act a certain way. These expectations drive us along toward our achievements. In fact, they determine what it is we will achieve. They determine what our priorities will be.

The same is true of your children. If you believe your children will disappoint you or not perform, they will probably "live down to" your expectations. On the other hand, your children will also rise to your expectations if you believe they have the ability to achieve and you encourage them along the way.

The Bible emphasizes hating the sin but loving the sinner. Some parents, though, indicate a contempt for the sinner—their children: "Why'd you do that? *What an idiot!*" "Sometimes you are so out of line *it's like you just want trouble.*" "I told you not to do that! *You're such a troublemaker!*"

You are an idiot; you want trouble; you are a trouble-maker. With "compliments" like that, don't be surprised when that child lives down to the parents' expectations.

This is all about self-fulfilling prophecies. You prophesy that your child will achieve or fail at something. Your expectation determines the way you respond to your child's attempts at that goal. It is your response that has a lot to do with your child's achievement.

One study done by educational researchers on how a parent's response to report cards affected the child's grades is enlightening. They found that children whose parents showed too much concern and were never satisfied, or children whose parents showed little concern and conveyed a "do-the-best-you-can" attitude, did not improve their grades as well as those children whose parents praised good work, encouraged better performance, and assured the children that they could come to the parents for help.

If you want to raise your children to achieve great things, you need to frequently assure them that they are winners—that they have the ability to achieve. That frequent assurance needs to be more than just "baseball chatter." You know what that is: "Come on, Billy Bob!" "You can do it now, big guy." Rather, I mean, look into their eyes, give them a *specific affirmation,* and then take a very important step: Let them soak it up. Let your children feel how good it is to be affirmed specifically.

I.Q. tests and achievement tests are fallible. They may be inaccurate, misleading, or misinterpreted. So be cautious about accepting pronouncements about your children's intelligence, aptitude, or potential. Nevertheless, expect achievement from your children, encourage them that they have the ability to achieve, then stand back and watch them take off.

TYRANT OR COACH?

You are not being a tyrant if you make your child do his homework over because of sloppy work. If you are firm, fair, gentle, and consistent in your insistence to redo the assignment, you are sending an important message to your child. You are conveying to him that *you believe* he can do better. You expect greater things because you see it in him.

A teacher once gave a simple writing assignment. Each student was to write one page on what he or she would want to do on a vacation. One student handed in a paper with only a one-sentence answer on it. Instead of giving the child a well-deserved failing grade, the teacher returned the paper with this message at the top: "I know you can do better than that, do it over."

The second draft of the assignment was handed in. This time it was a short paragraph sloppily written. The teacher returned it again, with these words: "You're beginning to show me what I knew you had all along. Fill the page and make it neater. No grade. Do over."

The third draft came in with the entire page filled, but the handwriting was still sloppy. The teacher wrote at the top: "I really like your story. Now, clean up your handwriting. No grade. Do over."

Finally the assignment came back perfectly up to standard: one full page neatly written. "Well done," the teacher wrote. "I knew you had it in you. 'A plus!' "

Unfortunately, some teachers (and parents) think that a child's self-esteem is damaged by expecting excellent work from him even when he is capable of it. In a previous chapter I told the story of the student in a school near Erie, Pennsylvania. His father showed me a two-page history report for which the boy had received an A. In the report totaling only eighty-one lines, the tenth-grade student had made 144 spelling, grammar, and punctuation errors! The teacher wrote at the top, "Good report and well written." When confronted by the parent, the teacher explained his grading by saying, "I didn't want to damage the boy's self-esteem." The teacher sent a clear message to the student, "You aren't capable of better work. Don't try." So much for enhancing his self-esteem.

To get a better feel for what was once expected of children, just consider what was required of rural, eighth-grade students in Kansas in 1900. Paul Roberts of the Center for Strategic and International Studies points out that in order to pass the eighth grade, students had to score well on numerous rigorous questions. The following questions are just a sampling of the test:

1. Spell "abbreviated," "elucidation," "assassination," and "animosity."
2. Make a table showing the different sounds of all vowels as well as "oo," "g," and "c."
3. Divide into syllables and mark diacritically the following words: profuse, retrieve, rigidity, defiance, priority, remittance, and propagate.
4. Find the interest on an 8 percent note for $900 running two years, two months, and six days.
5. Compare and contrast the various writings of Thomas Jefferson.
6. Name two countries producing large quantities of wheat, two of cotton, two of coal, two of tea; name three important rivers in the United States, three in Europe, three in Asia, three in South America, and three in Africa.
7. Analyze and diagram this sentence: "There is a tide in affairs of men, which taken at the root, leads on to fortune." That was followed by the requirement to parse "tide which taken leads."
8. Name the principle political questions which have been advocated since the Civil War and the party which advocated them.

9. Give a brief account of the colleges, printing, and religion of the colonies prior to the American Revolution.
10. Name the principal campaigns and military leaders of the Civil War.

THE POWER OF LOW EXPECTATIONS

One of the biggest problems facing young people today is society's expectations of them. Parents as well as educators simply do not expect excellence from students, morally or academically. It would appear that, regarding education, some adults put more of an emphasis on self-esteem than on academic success. Ironically, academic failure will eventually lead to low self-esteem.

One mother wrote me with her story about how high and low expectations affected her performance as a student. While in the ninth grade, her algebra teacher seemed to have something against girls who studied math. He constantly complained that girls were terrible at math and he would ridicule any girl who did poorly on a test. The woman wrote that she struggled to pass with a D. The next year she had another algebra class. The first day, the teacher greeted her with a smile and made her feel welcome. The teacher put the student's name on the board every time she got an A on an assignment. Everything was positive. Every word was encouraging. She passed the course with an A.

Parental expectations of students are also low. A New York City high school teacher who got frustrated at being blamed for being too lenient with his students toughened his standards. He later wrote: "My first-period students were absent an average of 27.5 days and late 11.7 times out of about eighty days of instruction. And when I did my duty and failed sixteen out of twenty-eight of them for the next-to-last report, how many parents stormed the gates of the school to investigate their kids' problem? Only one. And no parents called to investigate the reasons why I had failed students in my courses, though I failed a total of 111 in five classes."

The same problem with low expectations is found in how we teach children moral behavior in school. Most sex education courses expect that young people will be sexually active. Is it any wonder that the children live down to the educators' expectations? I once was asked to speak at the national convention of physician assistants. I spoke on "Adult Hang-ups in Teaching Sex to Kids." Many of those in my audience were surprised when, instead of talking about the failure of parents, I spoke of the failure of teachers to raise higher moral expectations. Afterward, some people approached me in disbelief. "These kids are having sex already!" they said. "Kids are also skipping school," I responded. "But do you teach them how to be truant and not get caught? No, you expect good behavior."

A teacher once contacted my office and told how a liberal sex education "expert" had lectured her class on contraceptive use. The visitor left the class with the impression that all teenagers were regularly having sex. The teacher was upset about the low moral expectation offered to the kids. The next day the teacher explained to the class that she was going to conduct an anonymous poll with two questions: Have you ever had sexual intercourse and do you plan on having sex before marriage? She collected the answers and tabulated the results on the chalkboard. None of the teenagers had had sex and only five planned on having sex before marriage. One boy approached the teacher afterward and thanked her for doing the poll. "I thought I was weird because I hadn't had sex," he explained.

SUMMARY
The powerful force in human relationships is expectations. Expect great things from young people. Encourage them toward excellence, both academically and morally. Then stand back and watch them take off. We adults often think that the biggest thing teenagers want is free-

dom, when actually it is guidance they crave.

Anchoring Questions for Chapter Eight:

1. What will you teach your child about why high expectations are important?

2. How will you model having high expectations for yourself?

3. In what area is your child meeting high expectations for which you can encourage him?

Orchestrate Success in
Your Child's Life

➤————————————————————————➤

Navigating Principle #9: Many children must be guided
to the realization that they are capable of achieving.

➤————————————————————————➤

Success breeds success. But underachieving children
lack success. It is most important that they achieve.
That is when it is necessary to orchestrate success.
This does not mean letting your child win artificially. It
means creating an environment in which your child can
truly achieve.

Many children learn to accept low achievement because they lack evidence in their lives that they can
achieve more. These underachieving children have to be
guided to the realization that they can achieve. The key
word is *guided.* It means leading them to see the joy and
satisfaction in small successes.

A child acquires confidence in his power to succeed in
stages. You must guide him through those stages.
Achievement rarely happens by accident. Achievers plot
out how they are going to achieve. They set goals for

themselves. They have a plan of action.

Underachievers, on the other hand, rarely plot out anything. They tend to "float" through life. An underachieving child may be afraid to set a goal because that sets a standard by which he can be measured. The chance of failure increases. In his mind, if he has no goals, he can avoid accountability.

The attainment of a goal, however small, provides an opportunity for a child to acquire an inner sense of satisfaction and self-confidence. We have already gone over how to help your child set realistic goals. Let's strategize toward guiding your child to success.

Your child has *something* in which he or she is interested. It may be a hobby, a sport, an academic subject, or an activity. Think for a moment what that area of interest is and write it on a piece of paper.

Next, create a goal that you know your child would like to accomplish and write it down. Then, write down four or five action steps toward reaching the goal.

Finally, select an inner quality that will be exhibited by your child as he completes each step. As your child accomplishes each action step, praise him and encourage him in the quality he exhibited.

Example:
Identify one area in which your child shows interest.
Specific Area: Cooking.
Goal: To cook an entire Sunday dinner for the family.
Step 1: Decide what would make a great meal.
Step 2: Shop for all the proper ingredients.
Step 3: Follow the recipes carefully.
Step 4: Arrange the food artistically on the serving plates.

Decide on an inner quality that will be exhibited by your child as he or she completes each step. Refer to the inner qualities listed on page 108.
Quality Exhibited by Step 1: Imaginative
Quality Exhibited by Step 2: Organized

Quality Exhibited by Step 3: Conscientious
Quality Exhibited by Step 4: Artistic

Start with your child's area of interest. You can do this several times and take several weeks to complete it. Remember, the point of this exercise is to instill confidence in your child. Get him to believe he has the inner qualities necessary to achieve. Nothing stimulates the desire for success more than the experience of success. An underachieving child needs to start experiencing success.

A suspension bridge over a waterfall can be built by starting with a string. A man flys a kite across the falls and lets the kite come down on the opposite side. He then attaches a little heavier twine to the kite string and a man on the other side pulls it across. A thicker cord is attached to that and pulled across. Each time the cord gets thicker until it is a rope; then a cable; then a thick cable; then two cables, and so forth until a strong bridge is built.

That is like building your child's confidence. From small, easy things, to the final goal. After you and your child feel comfortable with setting goals in areas of interest, focus on an area of underachievement.

Your child doesn't need to see that you have preplanned your encouragement and praise as he accomplishes each step. This isn't manipulation, this is orchestrating success.

WHAT TO DO WITH THEIR FAILURES
The famous motivational speaker, Zig Ziglar, once commented: "Knowing how to benefit from failure is the key to success." Let's face it, life has many difficulties. Somehow we speak of "the good life" as if there is a point at which life becomes easy. If we hold that mentality very long we will get terribly frustrated. Failure is all around us just waiting to consume us. It is how we handle failure that is the key to success. A child needs to learn that simple principle early in life.

The opportunity to confront and overcome barriers is essential to the development of a child's self-confidence and self-image. Frustration can be a great tool . . . if used constructively. Frustration teaches a child something important about life: Achievement requires work. As one psychiatrist has observed: "Without frustration there is no need, no reason to mobilize your resources to discover that you may be able to do something on your own."

Allowing a child to experience a controlled amount of frustration is good. But that is different from allowing him to experience continual frustration and inescapable defeat. The right amount of frustration can cause a child to dig deep and mobilize his talents, skills, and discipline to achieve. Too much frustration, too much failure, can breed a feeling of hopelessness.

Parents have a powerful, natural instinct to protect their children from pain. If you have concluded your child is incapable of achieving in a certain area, you will tend to discourage your child from exposing himself to inevitable failure. However, you need to be careful that your child does not learn what one educational consultant calls "learned helplessness."

Learned helplessness is when a child perceives himself as incompetent and resigns himself to that perception. Playing the helpless role draws attention, sympathy, and support. Behavior patterns of children who have learned helplessness include chronic forgetfulness, sloppiness, or appearing dense.

The child who has learned helplessness must be convinced that he can survive without resorting to helplessness. His parents must create environments in which the "helpless" child can succeed alone. So you need to be careful not to protect your child from all frustration and failure.

When your child fails, first evaluate if he really did fail. Did your child fail or just fall short of your expectations? A child may think he did great on something until his parents look at it and declare "failure" based on an unre-

alistic expectation. Periodic introspection is important to
see if we are imposing our fantasies on our children. Are
you a perfectionist? Do you expect perfection from your
child?

Many parents identify so strongly with their child's
goals and achievements that they see the child's failure
as a personal failure. A parent's perception of a child can
profoundly influence the child's perceptions of himself.
This goes back to the idea of self-fulfilling prophecies. If
you see your child as a failure, he may very well prove
you right.

Do you want to know what one of the most damaging
phrases in the world is when your child fails? It is, "I
told you so." Those four words convey a very pointed
message: "You failed!" If a child thinks he has let down
the people most important in his life, he may be tortured
by unnecessary guilt. The fear of failure is often more
harmful and hindering than the failure itself. The fear of
failure may inspire him or paralyze him.

Children need the courage to be imperfect. They need
to try new things without the fear that they will fail.
They need to try without fear that their failure will be
rubbed in by the people they love most. A child who has
become accustomed to frustration and defeat frequently
conditions himself not to reach beyond his self-imposed
boundaries.

Failure moves us closer to success . . . if we learn from
our mistakes and keep trying! We must be willing to
learn how *not* to do it if we want to spring back from
failure. People mocked Thomas Edison trying unsuccess-
fully some 5,000 materials for the filament of his great
dream, the incandescent light bulb. "You failed 5,000
times," said a critic of his day. "I have not failed," coun-
tered Edison. "I have discovered 5,000 materials that
won't work."

Over a hundred years ago, when Gail Borden, American pioneer and inventor, was crossing the Atlantic from
England, two children on board ship died because the milk

was contaminated. He began to dream of a way to make milk safe for shipboard use. He tried and tried but failed every time. Eventually he discovered a way through a principle called "condensed milk." When Mr. Borden died, his gravestone carried this epitaph: "I tried and failed. I tried again and again and succeeded." Our children need to learn that failure moves us closer to success . . . if we learn from our mistakes and keep trying.

COMMON SOURCES OF FAILURE

Failure can occur for many reasons. When analyzing why your child is failing, you need to consider a few common sources.

1. The task is too difficult. It could be that what your child is attempting *is* too difficult. This is where a reasonable amount of comparison can be good—how does your child compare to other children his or her age who are doing the same thing and have similar abilities.

2. Your child is ill-equipped for the task. It could be that your child has not learned the necessary skills to perform a particular task. For instance, your child may want to be on an athletic team. He or she may have the ability but may not be in proper shape and thus, fails to make it. In academics, your child may be sitting in an advanced class but has not built up the knowledge necessary to perform well. Being ill-equiped is being unnecessarily vulnerable to failure.

3. Your child may have relational problems. If your child is experiencing a strain in some relationship, whether it is family, friends, or teachers, that may affect his performance.

It is an established fact that if parents are having marital problems and the children sense it, their schoolwork goes downhill. One study done with families of high achievers found that a stable family environment was one of the most significant contributing factors in the children's achievement.

4. Your child may have emotional problems. We

have already looked at how fear can paralyze a child's performance. Your child's failure may arise from insecurity, fear, anger, or depression. It is important that you keep in touch with your child's feelings.

5. Your child may have learning problems. It may be that your child needs more than just adequate preparation for a task. He may need remedial training in reading, writing, studying, concentration, or comprehension. You need to examine the actual aptitudes your child has that are necessary to learn. The learning problem may run deeper and actually be a learning disability.

LEARNING DISABILITIES

A learning disabled child has a disorder in one or more of the basic psychological processes involved in understanding or in using language, spoken or written. It can manifest itself in a hampered ability to listen, think, speak, read, write, spell, or do math. This is more than just poor study habits or lack of practice in something like penmanship.

A learning disability involves something going on in the brain that causes a person to process information incorrectly or not at all. There are many symptoms of a learning disability. A few include:

1. Short attention span
2. Poor memory
3. Difficulty following directions
4. Trouble discriminating between letters, numbers, or sounds
5. Consistently inappropriate responses
6. Restless and easily distracted
7. Saying one thing and meaning another
8. Inability to follow multiple directions

Because of these disabilities children can easily become discouraged, unmotivated, or rebellious. If we do not recognize their learning disability, we often treat them inappropriately. We punish them or push them or praise them—but we never cure them.

A child with a learning disability often has above average intelligence—he's bright—but he can't perform well. It is like being a brilliant artist but having your arms tied behind your back. You want to do well. You know you *can* do well, but you just can't seem to get it out.

What to Do

If you feel your child is learning disabled, and many children are, don't hesitate to seek help.

1. Have him tested by a school psychologist. Public schools have psychologists available who can test children for learning disabilities. This is not the same as putting your child in therapy. A school psychologist has several tests to determine academic aptitudes and learning problems. If you are home schooling or have your child in a private school, you may have to go to a child psychologist to be tested.

2. Your child needs to take three tests: an I.Q. test, an achievement test, and a personality test. These tests will start to pinpoint your child's need.

3. Get special instruction through your school or through a private tutor. Your school psychologist can make appropriate recommendations.

Again, this is for when you suspect that your child has a disability that is causing him or her to process information incorrectly. This is a learning disability and can generally be treated with the right kind of help.

A Checklist

This checklist, developed by Lawrence Greene of the Development Learning Center, will not tell you what to do, but it may help you identify a reason for a particular failure. It is a place to start when analyzing your child's situation.

1. My child's peers, as a group, are struggling with this task.   yes   no

2. My child's teacher sees this task as reasonable for my child.   yes no

3. My child has gone through the necessary training for this task.   yes no

4. My child has been provided with the proper tools to perform the task.   yes no

5. My child's reading skills are good.   yes no

6. My child's study habits are good.   yes no

7. My child retains most of what he/she reads.   yes no

8. Our family environment is stress-free.   yes no

9. I spend a good amount of time with my child.   yes no

10. My child watches less than one hour of television each night.   yes no

11. My child has good, close friends.   yes no

12. My child's friendships are going well right now.   yes no

13. My child has a good rapport with his/her teacher.   yes no

14. I *know* my child is free from unusual amounts of fear, anxiety, insecurity, anger, or depression.   yes no

Focus on any statement with which you answered no. It may indicate a factor influencing your child's failure at this time.

Here are some points to remember in helping your children deal with failure.

1. Love them for who they are, not for how they perform. Be sure you communicate your love to them.
2. Express your belief in their ability to achieve.
3. Focus on a good quality they exhibited in their effort to achieve.
4. Remind them that life is hard and that achievement takes special effort.
5. Point out that each time we fail, we learn something about how *not* to do it.
6. During all this, look for any possible underlying reasons for their failure and act appropriately.

MYTHS OF SUCCESS

When the subject of success and failure is discussed, it is important to address three common myths of success. I don't know how these myths got started, but somehow they have crept into our thinking and hold us back from really achieving or at least they hold us back from enjoying our achievement because we can never *feel* like we are successful. The three myths are: (1) the myth of perfection; (2) the myth of finality; and (3) the myth of comparison.

The Myth of Perfection

Often we view success as perfection. This myth causes us to think, "Success means I'm achieving perfectly." Logically, of course, this is impossible. But often, we hold this myth deep inside us. We are never satisfied with our achievement because it is not perfect. The myth of perfection causes us to focus on how many times we fail rather than how many times we succeed.

In 1927, Babe Ruth hit 60 home runs, more than anyone in the history of baseball to that time. He also set another record that year: He struck out more than anyone in the history of baseball! In baseball, a player who

bats a consistent .400 would be considered a great athlete. Yet, that also would mean he is consistently making
outs 60 percent of the time.

People who lack the courage to be imperfect are hampered in many everyday events. They are afraid to try
something new—to venture out. A successful business-
man once said, "Anything worth doing is worth doing
poorly—until you learn to do it well."

In 1928 Paul Galvin, at the age of thirty-three, had
failed miserably in business once already and his second
attempt—the manufacturing of storage batteries—went
belly up. Convinced he had a product with tremendous
potential, he attended the auction of his own business
and, with $750 he scraped together, he bought back one
portion of it. That was the beginning of Motorola.

The myth that success means perfection creeps into
how we rate ourselves and others around us including
our family. Oftentimes we expect perfection from our
children. It is important that we see our children as people with tremendous abilities and opportunities and allow them to develop gradually.

Perseverance is a key to achievement. Perseverance
comes through accepting imperfection. Discouragement
and quitting set in when we seek perfection and lose it.
Life is full of stumbling blocks and those who achieve
learn how to go over them or around them. Perseverance
requires patience. Listen to the Apostle Paul's letter to
his student, Timothy, in 1 Timothy 1:15-16:

Here is a trustworthy saying that deserves full acceptance: Christ Jesus came into the world to save
sinners—of whom I am the worst. But for that very
reason I was shown mercy so that in me, the worst
of sinners, Christ Jesus might display His unlimited
patience as an example for those who would believe
on Him and receive eternal life.

Paul, probably the most successful Christian in history, wasn't perfect. He said, "I am the worst" among sinners. Notice how patient God was with Paul. Paul says God dealt mercifully and patiently with him. God deals mercifully and patiently with our children. Even so should we. Success does not mean perfection.

The Myth of Finality

This is the idea that success is a point rather than a process—the idea that there is a finality, an end point. We are captured by this myth when we think, "I made it" rather than "I am making it."

Can you imagine trying to evaluate a stockbroker by how his choice of stocks did on any given day? One day he is a failure, the next day he is a success, the next day he is a failure, and so on. Instead, you have to look at his record over a longer period of time.

Some people look at their children's situation and sadly think, "He is a failure" or "She'll never really make it" because they can't seem to arrive at that arbitrary and subjective point we've determined is "success." Achievement is a process, not a point. A successful lifestyle is much more important than a successful moment.

Child development experts emphasize that some children who lag behind developmentally are simply slow starters. The "late bloomer" is simply a person who achieved more than we thought he could because we labeled him "slow." In young children it is not the lagging behind that should be of concern as much as the danger emotionally that always being behind may cause.

What did Paul say about his reaching a point of achievement? In Philippians 3:12 after talking about his pursuit of a successful lifestyle, he says, "Not that I have already attained all this, or have already been made perfect." But what did he do? "I press on" (v. 14).

The Myth of Comparison

This is the tendency to rate your child's success by comparing him or her to others. We need to be careful about comparing our children to others.

Sometimes the logic behind rating our children's success by comparing them to others is that such a comparison will act as an inspiration or maybe incite competition. Many times it can create feelings of self-doubt, discouragement, and inadequacy in a child.

It is important to remember that achievement is no guarantee of happiness. One educational consultant has observed that compulsive overachievers are not necessarily happier or better adjusted than those who are less driven. Yet often these compulsive overachievers become our heroes and role models. We admire their accomplishments, but rarely do we look at their personal lives. The trail to the summit of success is strewn with shattered relationships, abandoned families, self-centered intoxication, and physical and emotional self-abuse.

The Terman Study, started in the 1920s, followed the lives of 1,500 high-I.Q. California schoolchildren. Though they did generally better in careers than their peers throughout life, the group produced no creative or artistic geniuses. No Einsteins or Picassos. In other words, a high I.Q. does not mean success.

Different is not better or worse—it's just different. School can be agonizingly eye-opening for many children. They are thrust into a group of their peers where oftentimes their friends are more athletic, better spellers, more artistic, or better looking. In a home where success is measured by comparison, little Johnny or little Suzy are given the tools, not to build their own ladders, but to dig their own holes.

When a child's achievement is continually being measured in comparison to others, the message being sent is, "You're not good enough." You can always find someone who is better than you are at something. You can always find someone who is worse than you.

Being different is what makes you *you!* No two children are alike, and that's what makes them special. They are unique treasures of God.

Is all comparison bad? No. We are constantly comparing ourselves with others to see if we are normal. Comparing your child with others is perfectly normal and it is one way of sensing when something is wrong (or right).

If your child is struggling at something that his classmates find easy, there may be something wrong. Some comparisons are fine. But belittling a child by comparison can be devastating.

It's easy to compare our children to other people. To help identify how you may be doing this, read the following exercise and write your answers on a piece of paper. First is a list of *people* you may find yourself comparing your children to:

Brother	Sister	A friend's child
Cousin	You (your childhood)	A child on TV
Their friends	Jesus Christ	Classmates

Next is a list of *qualities* you may be comparing:

Athletic	Musical	Artistic
Intelligence	Good reader	Good at math
Obedience	Attitude	Generosity
Neatness	Kindness	Responsibility
Hard worker	Academics	Articulation

Now, think about your child and what you may be comparing and to whom you may be comparing him or her. Make a list using the categories shown below.

Your Child	*Quality*	*Compared to Whom*
_____	_____	_____
_____	_____	_____
_____	_____	_____

Periodic introspection is good for understanding how

you are responding to your child. Shirley Gould, in her book *The Challenge of Achievement,* points out that parents who feel inadequate about themselves may have a tendency to prove their value through their children. They never amounted to much so they try to live vicariously through their children's accomplishments.

The superimposing of a goal onto a child may end in disaster. For example, a child may have excellent mathematical aptitude and the parents conclude he should be an engineer. However, the child also may enjoy music, yet he dutifully goes on to become a successful engineer and, thus, fulfill the dreams of his parents. At age forty he realizes he hates engineering and decides to quit to become a musician. His wife and friends conclude he is going through mid-life crisis.

One educational consultant specializing in work with underachievers has commented, "Resist the temptation to impose your fantasies on your child." Instead, encourage your child to establish goals compatible with his or her talents and interests and to achieve in those areas. Of course, if you are convinced your child's underachievement is wasting valuable abilities that he or she will regret later in life, you need to intervene.

Knowing when to do that is an art, not a science. I certainly can't tell you when it is right or wrong. That is why I suggest periodic introspection to figure out what it is you do expect from your child and most importantly, *why.* You may be comparing your child to your own fantasy.

SUMMARY

Many children must be guided to the realization that they are capable of achieving. This will involve helping them have small successes and lavishing praise and encouragement on them. It is important that the underachieving child learn to bounce back from failure. Thoughtful analysis may help you determine why your child failed and what path to take to help him succeed.

While working with your child it is important to keep in mind the three myths about success that may be preventing growth. Helping your child develop means playing the part of a loving coach. This means having a conscious plan of action for providing the environment for your child's success.

Anchoring Questions for Chapter Nine:

1. Which of the three myths of success could your child be struggling with and what will you teach him about it?

2. How will you model the proper attitude toward success in countering the myth your child may be struggling with?

3. Which of the three myths of success is your child not struggling with and how will you encourage him to continue having the right attitude toward success?

Build a Safe Harbor
for Your Child at Home

➤――――――――――――――――――――――――――――➤

Navigating Principle #10: The parents' role in creating a home environment of success is a key to helping your child succeed.

➤――――――――――――――――――――――――――――➤

One of the most beautiful sights to a weather-weary sailor is a safe harbor. A friend and his wife had the adventure of their lives when they decided to spend five years sailing alone throughout the Caribbean. Many times they ran into violent storms and would have to tie themselves to the helm so they could steer their boat and not be blown overboard. The rain poured so heavily they couldn't see the bow of their small vessel. All they could do was ride out the storm and wait for better weather. Once, calm weather didn't come for twelve days. For twelve days they barely slept and remained strapped to the helm of the boat. Oh, how they wished for a safe harbor. Your child needs a safe harbor from the storms of life surrounding him too.

A country philosopher once said, regarding the importance of time: "The best inheritance parents can give their children is—a few minutes of their time each day." The quality *and* quantity of time parents spend with their children is of vital importance in building a safe harbor at home.

Many "upwardly mobile" parents think that the quantity of time is not as important as the quality of time. But the facts don't support that reasoning. One study involving 2,400 fifth-graders found that the one thing they found *most* upsetting was spending too little time with their parents.

Alan Ginsberg, Director of Planning and Analysis for the Department of Education, has cited that working mothers during the weekday spend only about eleven minutes in educational pursuits with their children and only about twenty-three minutes per day over the weekend. Ginsberg also found that children whose mothers work outside the home tend to do worse in school than do kids of mothers who stay at home.

American mothers on average spend less than half an hour a day talking, explaining, or reading with their children. Fathers spend less than fifteen minutes doing the same.

When you think you don't have time to spend with your child, you should remember that twenty-five years from now your TV set will still be there and your favorite show will be on re-runs, but your son or daughter's formative years will be gone *forever.* Which can you least afford to miss? Have you ever heard anyone in their latter years look back on life and say, "Boy, I wish I'd put more time in at the company?" Have you ever heard anyone say, "I wish I'd watched more TV?"

Zig Ziglar points out that two of the saddest words in life are: "If only . . ." What despair! What hopelessness! "If only I had spent more time . . ." "If only I had encouraged him more . . ." "If only I had known what he was going through. Things could have been different!"

Instead of saying, "If only . . ." say, "Next time . . ." You can turn despair into opportunity. "Next time, I will

spend more time ..." "Next time, I will encourage
him ..." Instead of, "If only I knew going to his game
was so important to him." Make it, "Next time he has a
game, I'll be there!" We all have opportunities for "Next
time." Today you can turn all the "if onlys" into "next
times."

FINDING TIME

Time is no respecter of persons. Everyone gets twenty-
four hours to live each day. The question is not whether
you have enough time, but how you use your time. A
good way to rethink how you use the time God has given
you is to simply track it for one week.

On a piece of paper, write the days of week across the
top and the hours of the day down the left side.

	Mon.	Tues.	Wed.	Thurs.	Fri.	Sat.	Sun.
6 A.M.							
7 A.M.							
8 A.M.							
9 A.M.							
10 A.M.							
11 A.M.							
12 P.M.							
1 P.M.							
2 P.M.							
3 P.M.							
4 P.M.							
5 P.M.							
6 P.M.							
7 P.M.							
8 P.M.							
9 P.M.							
10 P.M.							
11 P.M.							

Twice a day (at lunch and before bed) reflect on how you

spent the previous hours. Write down what you did with each hour. After you've done that, see where you have spent time with your children and see if anything unnecessary is interfering with it. Count up the number of hours you spend watching TV during the week. If it's under ten, you are doing great.

How much time do you spend reading *anything* at home? How much time do you spend in church-related activities? Do you eat breakfast and dinner as a family? Draw a star in the time slots you *could* adjust to spend more time with your children. As you do that, think of times you could spend reading to or conversing with your children.

I was talking one day with the family ministries pastor of a very large church in Southern California about the *Charting* seminar. He was very interested in having it presented at his church until I mentioned that it emphasizes having family time together at least once a week. "I don't even do that with my family," he blurted out. "That's impossible in today's world with teenagers." He went on to explain that Sundays are filled with church services, Mondays the kids concentrate on homework, Tuesdays his wife teaches a Bible study, Wednesdays he has church meetings, Thursdays he teaches a Bible study, Fridays the kids have youth activities, and Saturdays they go out on their own. This family ministries pastor described his own schedule in such a way as to show that he never had any time with his family!

TIME ASSESSMENT

Another way to evaluate how you use your time is to rate yourself on specific time-consuming activities. Draw a horizontal line on a piece of paper and mark it with lines to create a scale from one to seven. Label the number one with "too little time," the number four with "about right," and the number seven with "too much." Next, list the following twelve activities and rate them on the seven-point scale (note: TV doesn't quite fit the scale

because you can never watch too little of it). (1) TV viewing, (2) Reading books, (3) Reading periodicals/newspapers,
(4) Reading aloud to your children, (5) Church activities,
(6) Planned family activities, (7) Meals eaten together,
(8) Time with children's schoolwork, (9) Time spent playing or working with your children, (10) Hobbies and
recreation, (11) Time spent on your job, (12) Special
planned times with your spouse.

Focus on the areas in which you rated yourself with a
six or seven (too much) and a one or two (too little).
Come up with a few goals for regaining balance in your
life. You may find that you are spending too much time
on a hobby and neglecting your family. You may find you
are spending too little time creating memories with your
spouse.

BASIC ACHIEVEMENT TOOLS
There are three simple things you can start doing today
that will give your child an "edge" at school. With these
three activities you can give to your child the tools for
achievement that many children, unfortunately, do not
have. They are simply: conversation, questions, and
reading.

A study entitled, "The Disadvantaged Child and the
Learning Process" done by Martin Deutsch, found that
in homes where conversation, questions, and reading are
not encouraged, the child enters school significantly
short of the basic achievement tools. When compared to
his higher achieving classmates, he asks fewer questions,
uses shorter sentences, and has both a smaller vocabulary and a shorter attention span. All of that just because
Mom and Dad didn't devote larger quantities of time conversing with and reading to their children.

Conversations involve vulnerability. To have a conversation means that both people involved are willing to
learn something the other person knows. Unfortunately,
parent/child interaction often is only a monologue. The
parent is telling the child something. Certainly this type

of communication is important, but be sure to balance it with conversation.

Questions are important for discovery and learning. Questions are like keys that unlock doors. The right question can bring the right answer to open up whole worlds of understanding. Children need the opportunity to ask lots of questions and get substantive answers. It will contribute to their academic success because they learn to be curious. They learn to seek answers. They more readily ask questions in class.

Here's an example of the difference a well-placed question can make when talking with your child. When your child comes home from school and you ask, "How was your day?" the response from your child may often be, "Fine." The question was too open-ended. It didn't require any thinking on the part of the child. Next time try asking, "What was the most interesting thing you did today?" and don't let your child get away with answering, "Nothing." Other specific questions you could ask would be: "What is one thing you learned in history (or science, or English) today?" "What did you do today about which you felt good?" or, "What was the funniest thing you heard today?"

Reading is the most important tool for learning. If your child struggles at reading, he or she will struggle throughout school. Poor readers get frustrated easier and quit school. Reading opens windows to exciting worlds and fascinating discoveries. To be able to read is to be liberated from the confines of our own experience. We learn from others by reading what they have experienced, thought about, or learned. Reading is an intimate experience between the author and the reader. The world is improved one person at a time and, when you are reading an uplifting book, the focus is right where it should be: one on one.

Do not assume that because your children are in school they are learning to read well. There are a high percentage of illiterates in school today. Some school programs teach reading better than others. Casually test your children by having them read aloud to you. If your child struggles, begin tutoring him. The time you spend with your child will be the best investment you can make for his future.

INSTILLING A DESIRE TO LEARN

If anyone is ever going to achieve anything, he must have the desire to achieve. We have seen that achievement comes through three things: ability, effort, and desire.

There are two good ways to arouse your children's desire to learn:

1. *By having them see learning as a bridge to achieving the things they want.* Your child sets a goal and then strategizes a path to attaining that goal. The path may involve schoolwork, but the motivation to excel in school comes from keeping an eye on a particular, external goal.

2. *By helping them enjoy the discovery of new things.* Your child wants to learn and tolerates the work because the reward of discovery feels good.

HOW TO HELP YOUR CHILD BECOME INTERNALLY MOTIVATED

First, start with things about which your child is already internally motivated. What is your child interested in: sports, cars, dolls, outer space, airplanes, clothes? Next, figure out what academic area could somehow relate to that area of interest. Finally, strategize ways to build bridges between what your child is interested in and more academic subjects.

The following worksheet is designed to help you identify your child's interest, academic areas that relate to that interest, and how to bring the two together.

**Finding Your Child's Internal Motivation and
Relating It to Academics**

1. List two things in which your child is very interested.

2. From the list below, identify a few academic subjects
or activities that somehow could be related to your child's
two areas of interest:

Math	Chemistry	Reading	Writing
History	Biology	Physics	Geology
Geography	Anthropology	Zoology	Languages
Algebra	Geometry	Statistics	Sociology
Medicine	Engineering	Architecture	Fine Arts
Applied Arts	Music	Psychology	Aeronautics

3. Think of a person, a place, and a thing you have access
to that can act as a bridge between your child's interest
and the academic subject.

Academic Subject	*Person*	*Place*	*Thing*
Aeronautics	Pilot	Airport	Boeing 747
Math	Programmer	Office	Computer

At the bottom of the worksheet you should write in
someone you know who can talk to your child about his
interest, a place you can take your child that will spur his
interest, and a thing you can give him or show to him
that will help build a bridge between his interest and an
academic subject. Now your job is to bring those people,
places, and things into your child's life.

There are two things on the preceding list of subjects
that can be applied to any interest your child may have.
They are reading and writing. Your child can always read
about his or her area of interest and he or she can always
write something about it—a book report, an account of

an experience, or a creative story involving the area of interest. Reading and writing are two basic academic subjects that can be applied to any area of interest.

FOUR FACTORS FOR DOING BETTER IN SCHOOL

If your child is going to achieve in school, he or she must use the four basic factors. Let's call it the PLUS factor because it must be added to the other elements of achievement. We've looked at what success is and isn't. We've seen God's success ladder. We've seen the importance of setting goals and having self-discipline. We've seen the importance of self-confidence and encouragement. And we've seen the importance of reading and having a desire to learn.

To achieve in school your child must also add an extra factor—the PLUS factor. The PLUS factor has four parts.

P   = Paying attention
L   = Learning and remembering
U   = Upholding an interest
S   = Studying

"P"—Paying Attention

Your child has to pay attention to what is being taught. That is a simple fact. But how do you get kids to pay attention in class? It does little good to simply tell them to pay attention.

A child must see that paying attention is important. He must want to be attentive. That gets back to internal motivation—desire. One way to create motivation is to show your child that success in school opens up options—options for further schooling, career, and financial security. Another way to create desire is to help your child sense the good feeling associated with achievement. You may have to start small, but once he feels how good it is to achieve, he'll want more.

Another thing you can do to emphasize paying attention in class is to make good listening a game. Suggest to your child that he try to listen for and write down the teacher's main point and subpoints.

Make the game fun by having your child draw a tree trunk at the bottom of the page. Write the main point on the trunk. Then add branches to the trunk for each subpoint the teacher has. From each branch (subpoint) have your child attach "fruit" which are the specific facts associated with each point.

Each evening you can look at your child's "trees" and praise him or her for a job well done. Reward him with a small prize for each tree drawn. Have fun with it. Try drawing different kinds of trees.

Another game your child can play is "anticipation." This is played by trying to anticipate, then writing down what the teacher will talk about next. If the teacher talks about it, the child wins.

"L"—Learning and Remembering
Once your child is paying attention, the learning process can take place. Everybody has a particular learning style. Some people learn better by seeing information, others by hearing information, and others by handling information. We all use sight, sound, and touch to some degree, but we also lean toward a particular way of learning that emphasizes one over the other. There have been a lot of studies on learning styles. You can even take tests to determine your style of learning. Basically, learning styles can fall into six areas.

Learning involves receiving information and working with information. So, we can form two major categories for learning styles, each having three subcategories: (1) styles of reception, and (2) styles of production.

Styles of Reception
Your child receives information at school three ways:
1. Visually

2. Audibly
3. Tactilely
  Visual. A visual learner functions best by seeing
things. He likes pictures, graphs, diagrams, and reading
material. A visual learner should focus on taking notes,
drawing pictures, illustrating an abstract subject.
  Be sure to provide a visual learner with paper and
pencils, visual stimuli, and have him sit in class with a
clear view of the chalkboard and movie screen.
  Auditory. An auditory learner functions best by hearing information. He likes to listen and remembers things
heard on the radio or verbally explained in class. If an
auditory learner has trouble remembering material he
reads, he might try reading aloud into a tape recorder
and listening to himself. An auditory learner can be easily distracted by outside noises.
  Tactile. Tactile means to perceive by touching. A tactile learner functions best using a "hands-on" approach.
He can best remember information that he handles. A
tactile learner does well with acting out information in
skits and dramatic roles. Physical activity is important to
a tactile learner and he may need to *walk* through a
museum and *touch* the displays. A tactile learner learns
by "doing." For instance, a tactile learner will put a model together by "feeling" his way rather than reading the
instructions.
  To determine your child's learning style, you need to
observe how he or she processes information. Visually?
Audibly? Tactilely? Then, think of ways to help them
process their schoolwork using a visual, auditory, or tactile approach.

Styles of Production
The other major category of learning style is how your
child works with information. Once the information has
been received, how does your child work with it? This
covers study habits, group interaction, and how your
child works on projects.

The three areas of production styles are:
1. Relational
2. Directional
3. Independent

Relational. A relational learner likes to work in groups, participates well in class discussions, and feels most comfortable when interacting with others on projects. A relational learner is a good team player and sees himself as a contributing member of the group. He or she functions best in study groups and discussions. Being cooped up in a bedroom to study alone may be counterproductive for a relational learner.

Directional. A directional learner needs to know the "clear-cut rules of the game." He or she needs specific instructions: how many pages to write, what *exactly* is expected, and when he or she should study. A directional learner needs direction, often looks to others for guidance, and feels secure with the supervision of an authority figure.

Independent. An independent learner likes to work alone on a project, needs little direction, and is internally motivated. An independent learner is goal-oriented but has difficulty being a team player. He or she can function well with group interaction but does not need group approval. Adequate space and freedom are important to an independent learner and he will resent too much interference from others.

When it comes to learning and remembering, it is important to keep in mind your child's learning style. Ask yourself how your child receives information best: visually, audibly, or tactilely? Also, ask yourself how your child works with information best: relationally, directionally, or independently?

"U"—Upholding an Interest

Upholding an interest in school involves seeing the importance of being there, paying attention, learning, and remembering. If your child is going to see the importance of school, it must be meaningful to him.

A student should be able to answer why he or she is in a particular class. Often young people never think about why they go to school. To that question they might respond, "Because I have to" or, "Because I want to get a job." Education is not just for the purpose of earning a living. Education is learning what to do with a living after you earn it.

"Meaningfulness" can come from four major sources:

1. Enjoyment. Your child just may enjoy the subject or the environment. This is one of the best motivators. It means that your child truly enjoys learning for the sake of discovery or self-improvement.

2. Goals. Your child may understand that upholding an interest in the class will lead to a good grade, or making the team. If your child is older, he may understand that upholding an interest in class will lead to greater opportunities in college or in the job market. As your child establishes goals in various areas of his or her life, the meaningfulness of schoolwork will become more apparent.

3. Good friends. Positive pressure works well in creating meaningfulness in a subject. Any teacher can tell you that many children are motivated or "de-motivated" in academics by the friends they keep. If your child's friends are interested in a particular subject, he or she will often become interested too.

4. Your example. If you want your child to be interested in learning, *you* need to be interested in learning. Are you interested in what your child is learning? Usually, parents only want to know if the homework is done. This is not interest in the subject itself.

Find out what your child is learning. Read about it so you can interact with your child. Show some interest in the subject. If you are not interested in your child's school subjects, why should he be? He may conclude that since you aren't interested it must not be important.

Go beyond an interest in whether or not your child is

doing homework. Get interested in *the subject* of the homework. Your child is not doing homework for homework's sake. He is doing homework to learn a subject. So, get interested in the *subject!*

"S" – Studying

Finally, the "S" in PLUS stands for studying. It is unrealistic to think that your child will be able to achieve well in school without doing a good amount of outside studying or homework. Poor study skills go hand in hand with underachievement. We are going to look at a few ingredients for good study skills and then focus on one particular technique that your child will find helpful.

The basic ingredients of good study skills:

1. Setting specific goals. Have clear and precise study goals. This means going beyond the standard, "I will read ten pages of the textbook" but rather means having a specific goal such as, "I will be able to list the basic characteristics of a single cell." These goals can be determined by skimming the reading, looking at subheadings, and reading the questions listed at the end of the chapter.

2. Being organized. Give your child a calendar to write down due dates for homework.

3. Note-taking and outlining. Information given in class can be studied once it is clearly written down.

4. Concentration. The mind has several sensory "gates" such as the eyes and ears. If loud music is playing while your child is trying to read, his brain is constantly switching back and forth between the eye gate and the ear gate. It's best for your child to give his brain a rest by concentrating on one or the other. However, it has been shown that soft music helps block out other distractions while studying.

SQ3R

SQ3R stands for: Survey, Question, Read, Recite, and Review. The SQ3R method will help your child select what is important to know, comprehend rapidly, remember ideas, and review efficiently at a later time.

When given a textbook reading assignment, your child should first *survey* the material. Attention should be given to the introduction, chapter summary, and questions at the end. A textbook is not a novel. It's OK to read the end first. This acts as a "road map." Your child will get an idea of where he is going. It also enables him to formulate specific homework goals. When surveying the reading, he should also look at the subheadings and any charts, graphs, and pictures.

After your child has surveyed the reading and *before* actually reading the textbook, have him ask himself *questions.*

For example, if the subheadings are, "The Colonists in the New World," your child might ask: "Who were the colonists?" "Where did they come from?" "Why did they come to the New World?" "What is the New World?"

Your child can also use the questions at the end of the chapter to formulate questions. Have your child write down his questions and leave several lines for answers. Now your child is ready to actually read the textbook. At first it may seem like a lot more work to survey and ask questions. But reading the text will be easier because of it.

The first "R" in SQ3R stands for *read.* He should now read to answer his written questions. He needs to be an active thinker while reading. Just reading to "cover the ground" is monotonous and will lead to boredom. But reading to actively answer questions gives purpose to the exercise. When he finds the answers he should jot down brief notes, not whole sentences.

The second "R" in SQ3R stands for *recite.* At the end of the reading assignment, your child should then recite out loud to himself the major points of the chapter or the answers to his questions. Reciting should be in your child's own words. It should not just be rereading the material. When your child can put it in his own words it means he has understood it better.

Finally, the third "R" stands for *review*. Periodic review of the material is important. For instance, just before reading a new chapter your child may find it helpful to review the main ideas of the previous chapter. Not only does this prepare him for material that is most likely based on previous learning, but it also keeps the previous points fresh in your child's mind.

In 1898 a Dr. Ebbinghaus studied the retention rate of people trying to remember relatively meaningless, rote material. He found that twenty minutes after reading the material, people remembered less than 60 percent of it. After one hour they remembered only about 55 percent of the material. After one day they could only remember 35 percent of what they read. After one week they could only remember 25 percent of the material. The more meaning attached to the reading, the greater the retention.

SQ3R or surveying, questioning, reading, reciting, and reviewing helps the brain retain information longer and makes the learning process more interesting.

SUMMARY

Creating the home environment for success in school is crucial for your children. This involves spending time with your children, instilling in them a desire to learn, showing great interest in what they are learning, understanding their personal style of learning, and coaching them in good study skills. The ever-important qualities of love for and nurture of your children are demonstrated in these actions.

Anchoring Questions for Chapter Ten:

1. What will you teach your child about how his or her area of interest relates to an academic subject?

2. How will you model the importance of education to your child?

3. What good study habits is your child demonstrating that you can encourage?

How to Help Your Child Become a Better Reader

Navigating Principle #11: The best way for parents to help their children become better readers is to read to them.

The man strained to see if anything lay ahead of him as he steered his vessel through the thick blackness of night. Somewhere ahead of him, he knew, was the mouth of the harbor and safety. The sea chopped and tossed at the boat as the heavy winds tore into the sails. The weekend trip for relaxation had turned into a treacherous fight for his life. The night before, during a violent storm, his dear friend and skipper of the getaway excursion died when he was swept overboard and sank beneath the surface of the sea. Now the man was left alone to find his way back to safety. Unfortunately, he didn't know how to read the maps or compass that were available. Darkness had rolled in and made vision useless.

Without being able to read the necessary guidance equipment, the man clutched the compass in his hands like some lucky charm and prayed that he would make it through the night. The sudden jolt and crunch coming from under him ruined such hope. He simply stood in numbing wonder as the little boat gently rocked backward and twisted slowly to the left while it crawled onto the black jagged rocks. The deck of the boat pitched and threw the man into the water. Fortunately, the rocks told him he was near shore. A few hundred yards away he saw the light of a house go on as someone looked out to see what had just happened. The man, still tightly holding the useless compass, swam toward the light and to rescue. If only he could have read the chart, he would have steered the boat to safe harbor.

The U.S. illiteracy rate is four times higher than the Soviet Union's and five times higher than Cuba's. The U.S. Department of Education claims that 20 percent of adults are functionally illiterate (that is, they cannot read well enough to function adequately in our society). Another 34 percent are estimated to be only marginally literate. In other words, 54 percent of our nation falls somewhere along the lines from bad to worse. Even when people can read, the figures are dismal. In 1980, the California Department of Education polled 233,000 sixth-graders and found that nearly 7 out of 10 rarely read for pleasure. A Gallup Poll taken in the 1970s found that 82 percent of the elementary children polled had not read a book in the preceding month but had watched nearly 100 hours of television. The U.S. Department of Education reveals that in a recent study of fifth-graders' reading habits, 90 percent of the children were found to read books only four minutes a day or less. The same children, however, watch an average of three hours of television each day.

World Almanac and Book of Facts polled 4,000 American eighth-graders in 1981 and found that when asked, "Whom do you most admire or whom would you most want to be like when you grow up?" the children listed three athletes, the rest were entertainers, and Burt

Reynolds topped the list. There were no politicians, lawyers, doctors, scientists, writers, or business leaders on the list.

The U.S. Department of Education published a booklet entitled *What Works: Research about Teaching and Learning.* In that report they made this very simple yet often neglected point: "The best way for parents to help their children become better readers is to read to them." Reading aloud to your child, no matter how old or young, is the single best thing you can do to stimulate learning.

You can start reading to children the day you start talking to them. Shortly after birth you can begin reading to a child. Certainly he won't understand the words, but his brain is like a sponge soaking things up. He is absorbing the sound and rhythm of the language. And after all, reading is much more beneficial than the wonderful-but-nonsensical "koochie, koochie, koo." In those early years your child is building a vocabulary. He hears sounds and rhythms and most importantly *he is being conditioned to enjoy the experience of books* by being held and given attention.

There is no upper age limit at which you should stop reading to your children. Even adults enjoy being read to. Every evening millions of adults hurry to their favorite chair and relax as they are read aloud to for thirty or sixty minutes by the nightly news anchorman. He even uses pictures! And we are mesmerized.

The answer to the question of when reading aloud to your children should stop is never. The impact won't be as great on older children as it is on younger children but you'd be surprised how much all children enjoy being read to.

When I was a substitute teacher and the regular teacher did not leave me with a specific lesson plan, I would pull out my copy of *Sex, Love or Infatuation* by Ray Short. I would read the title to the high school kids and ask if they wanted me to read a few passages to them. Once they heard the word *sex* in the title, they most often said yes! So I began reading. Short's book offers fourteen objective ways to look at a budding romance and tell whether it is deep or shallow. The students in my classes had never heard of such a thing. To them infatuation and love were synonymous. I would read for the entire hour while the classroom of teenagers listened intently. By the last period of the day I even noticed that some kids had skipped their other classes to slip into my classroom and hear more about the differences between love and infatuation. They loved to be read to because it was relevant.

ADVANTAGES OF READING ALOUD

1. It stimulates a child's interest in a subject. Books open whole worlds to a person.
2. It aids in a child's emotional development. Being held in your arms will cause the younger child to feel secure and warm toward the experience of reading (and learning).
3. It stimulates a child's imagination. A child must picture the story as you are reading.
4. It improves a child's language skills and vocabulary. An increased vocabulary gives a person a greater capacity for thinking because you formulate thoughts by means of mental words. The principle ingredient of all learning and teaching is language. We typically use only about 1,800 different words each day. Books give us exposure to an expanded vocabulary.
5. It educates, entertains, explains, and inspires.
6. It causes a child to enjoy books and learning.

Ruth Love, former superintendent of Chicago Public Schools, once said: "If we could get our parents to read to their preschool children fifteen minutes a day, we could revolutionize the schools." One study conducted in Harlem found that twenty classes of seven-year-olds who were read to for twenty minutes a day for one year scored significantly higher on vocabulary and reading comprehension tests than did a control group that was not read to.

There is an amazing, true story about the incredible results of reading aloud to a child. Cushla Yeoman was born with chromosome damage which caused deformities of her spleen, kidneys, and her mouth. She had muscle spasms which prevented her from sleeping more than two hours at a time and prevented her from holding anything in her hand until she was three years old. She also had hazy vision beyond her fingertips.

From infancy to age three Cushla was diagnosed as mentally and physically retarded and doctors recommended that she be institutionalized. But her parents refused that verdict. Noticing Cushla's interest in picture books, they began reading fourteen books to her each day.

By age five, though she still had physical deformities, psychologists found her to be well above average in intelligence and a socially well-adjusted child. Of course, reading aloud to your child is not a panacea for all ills. But it is amazing what the mental and visual stimulation will do, as well as the physical attention a child receives from being read to.

Jim Trelease, author of *The Read-Aloud Handbook,* suggests that parents excite children about books using the same techniques that advertisers use to sell toys to children:

1. Send your message to the child when he or she is still at a receptive age.
2. Make sure the message has enough sparkle in it to catch and hold the child's attention.
3. Make the message brief enough to whet the child's appetite, to make him want to see and hear it again and again.

A key to successful read-aloud time is matching the right book with the right child and reading with a good attitude. Here are some points to remember about what books to choose:

1. Children under eighteen months need *uncomplicated, color* pictures. Plot is not essential.
2. Once a child can sit calmly to hear a story, choose books that encourage interaction.
3. Choose longer stories with chapters when your child asks you to keep reading once you've finished a short story.
4. Choose a wide variety of subjects depending on your child's interests.

Several studies have shown four main factors present in homes where children become early readers: (1) The child is read to on a regular basis; (2) A wide variety of printed material is available at home (books, magazines, newspapers, comics); (3) Paper and pencil are readily available for the child. Scribbling and drawing encourage early development in the written language; (4) The parents answered the child's endless questions, praised the child's efforts to read and write, took him to libraries, and wrote stories their child dictated to them.

THE IMPORTANCE OF CONVERSATION

The U.S. Department of Education uses five major studies to prove that the conversation that goes with reading aloud to children is as important as the reading itself. When children take part in a thought-provoking discussion of a story, they understand more clearly that the purpose of reading is to get information and insight, not just to decode the words on a page. When parents ask children only superficial questions about stories, or don't discuss the stories at all, their children do not achieve as well in reading as the children of parents who ask questions that require thinking and who relate the stories to everyday events.

For instance, after reading about Peter Cottontail, a superficial question would be, "What kind of vegetable grew in the field where Peter went?" A more thought-provoking question would be, "Why do you think Peter's mother didn't want him to go into the cabbage patch?"

"Why" questions are often the most thought-provoking. The question, "Why?" looks for reasons and causes rather than just facts (who, what, where, when, and how). The question, "Why?" will cause your child to read between the lines, and draw inferences from what was read. It goes beyond merely recalling facts and causes your child to reflect on the story. Stories do not just convey facts, they convey meaning.

If your child has low reading comprehension—that is, your child doesn't remember a lot of what was read—you can help by discussing the story before *and* after reading it. This works especially well with homework.

TIPS ON READING ALOUD

1. Reading aloud does not come naturally. To be successful you must practice.
2. Be expressive when you read. Change your tone of voice to fit the scene and character.
3. Adjust your pace to fit the story. Slow down during suspenseful parts and help build the suspense.
4. Read slowly enough for your child to build mental images of the story.
5. Read as often as you and your child like.
6. Set aside at least one traditional time of day for a story. It could be before bed, before school, or during lunch.
7. Allow time for discussion after reading. Don't quiz your child; rather, encourage thought-provoking interaction.
8. Don't use the book as reward for being good. Withholding the book then becomes a punishment and may build negative feelings toward reading.
9. Fathers should read as much as possible to their sons. Since most primary-school teachers are women, boys often associate reading with being feminine.
10. Listening is a skill that must be learned and practiced. It takes time.

11. Many children find it difficult to sit still while being read to. Provide them with paper, pencils, and crayons to keep their hands busy.
12. Be sure your children see you reading for pleasure. Get them excited about reading by getting excited about it yourself.
13. Show your love for books. Books are objects to be enjoyed; they bring pleasure. Show your children how much pleasure you get out of books.

The next time you read a story to your child, show your love for the book. Cradle it in your arms. Open it gently. Tell your child how much *you* enjoy the book. When you are finished reading it, gently place it on the bookshelf and say something like, "Let's put it right up here where we can read it again when we want to. It's such a lovely book."

SUSTAINED SILENT READING

A great way to make reading a regular part of your family is to begin having sustained, silent, reading time. The U.S. Department of Education has observed that on the average, schoolchildren spend between seven and eight minutes reading at school. Most time is spent on reading drills rather than just reading.

Set aside some time at home when everyone reads something. The older the children, the longer the sustained, silent reading. Start out with just ten minutes. Work up to fifteen minutes and then twenty. Never use it as a punishment, but rather as an enjoyable family activity.

TELEVISION: THE GREAT INTRUSION

A mother once told me of a friend who came to visit and brought her eight-year-old daughter. The little girl immediately went through every room in the woman's house in a vain attempt to find a television set. Quite sometime before, the host had decided that their house was going to be a TV-free home and had gotten rid of the set. The frustrated little visitor finally asked, "Where's the TV?" The woman replied that they didn't have one. "Well then, how do you watch it?" the little girl asked in disbelief. Six weeks later the same mother and child were again visiting. Once again the girl inspected every room in search of the TV. Returning to the host, she exclaimed, "If you don't have a TV, just what do you do?"

Let's consider some facts about television. Ninety-eight percent of homes in America have a TV set. Fifty percent of American homes have two or more sets. The average set is on for seven hours each day. Our nation's three-year-olds are now watching as much TV as the ten-year-olds—an average of thirty hours each week. This means that by the time a child enters first grade he has seen more than 5,000 hours of television. In 1985 the American Psychological Association took a position that there is a link between the mayhem on children's programs and aggressive behavior in children. The American Academy of Pediatrics' Task Force on Children and Television has stated that repeated exposure to TV violence can make children not only accepting of real-life violence, but more violent themselves. Read-aloud expert and author Jim Trelease points out several damaging effects of excessive television viewing:

1. TV is the direct opposite of reading: it shortens attention spans; it allows no time for reflection; it encourages passivity.
2. For a young child, TV is an antisocial activity, while being read to is a social interaction.
3. TV deprives a child of his most important learning tool: his questions. TV doesn't listen and it doesn't answer.
4. TV relies on pictures and emotions which is counter to classroom activity which relies on reading and thinking.
5. TV promotes "the easy way out." Few problems are thought through or worked through. A seventeen-

year-old has seen 350,000 commercials promoting
easy solutions. Commercials promote consumption,
not production. A teenager has seen 350,000 ads promoting "having" but not "earning."

6. TV inhibits vocabulary development. Studies show
   that TV helps build vocabulary in preschool children.
   Yet, it also inhibits vocabulary development in early
   grades. TV is conversational, not literary.

7. TV desensitizes children's sense of sympathy for suffering. One study has shown that you would have to
   see all thirty-seven of Shakespeare's plays in order to
   see the same number of violent acts (fifty-four) por-
   trayed in three evenings of prime-time television.

8. TV stifles the imagination. A story is imagined differently by each listener until a TV director puts *his*
   version on film. Then everyone sees it the same.

9. TV is a major obstacle to family harmony. In a 1980
   survey, the Roper Organization polled 4,000 men
   and women about the main causes of fights between
   husbands and wives. They found that money was the
   number-one cause for marital disharmony—TV was
   second.

10. TV demands instant adulthood from children. Cur-
    rent programming focuses on incest, murder, abor-
    tion, rape, homosexuality, corruption, and violence.
    Almost 6 million children between ages two and elev-
    en are still viewing TV at 10:30 P.M.—when the
    "more mature" subjects are shown. But it's not just
    what goes into your child's mind that is the problem.
    Even more damaging is what is *not* going into your
    child's mind.

Patty Rebek, director of the psychology program at De
Paul University in Chicago comments: "The problem
comes when they don't do anything else—when they
start missing out on other things because of the TV."
The *Medical Society Journal* puts it this way: "The primary danger of the television screen lies not so much in
the behavior it produces, as the behavior it prevents."

A humorous but true story about the paralyzing effects of television comes from Daytona Beach, Florida. A man confessed to burglarizing homes while residents sat absorbed by TV programs. The report goes on to state that Thursday appeared to be the big night, due to hits like "The Cosby Show," "Family Ties," and "Cheers." Some people would even go so far as yelling at their dogs to stop barking so they could hear the TV.

Paul Cooperman, president of the Institute of Reading Development, looks at the problem this way in his book, *The Literary Hoax:*

> Consider what a child misses during the 15,000 hours (from birth to age 17) he spends in front of the TV screen. He is not working in the garage with his father, or in the garden with his mother. He is not doing homework, or reading, or collecting stamps. He is not cleaning his room, washing the supper dishes, or cutting the lawn. He is not listening to a discussion about community politics among parents and their friends. He is not playing baseball or going fishing, or painting pictures. Exactly what does television offer that is so valuable that it can replace all of these activities?

Cooperman's remarks lay the groundwork for creative strategies for overcoming the TV set. You can offer something the TV can't—yourself. You are a living, loving human being. You can listen and respond to your child; your TV can't. You can catch a ball, bake cookies, wash the car, or play games with your child; your TV can't.

OVERCOMING THE TELEVISION SET

There are many strategies for controlling the amount of TV your children watch. Here are a few suggestions.

1. Develop a TV viewing calendar. At the beginning of each week use a TV guide and have each child choose what he or she wants to view. A good rule of

thumb: Watch only seven hours of TV each week. Having your children schedule their TV viewing accomplishes the following:
- It teaches discernment and discrimination. They must *think* about what they really want.
- It teaches time management.
- It teaches self-discipline.
- It helps you monitor what is watched.
- It puts TV in its rightful place. TV should be considered like a book — a storyteller — not a member of the family.

2. Watch at least half of the programs your child watches. This should be done both for monitoring purposes and for interaction about the subject. If your child sees an interesting show on nature or technology, you can use that as a springboard for discussion. Or since you know in advance what the show is about, you may want to have a good book or magazine article to give to your child.

Even the Saturday morning cartoons *can* be beneficial. Dr. Paul Borgman of Northwestern College and author of *TV: Friend or Foe?* points out that young children have difficulty understanding such abstract concepts as justice, morality, and perseverance. But cartoons graphically illustrate these concepts. Good triumphs over evil. Justice is rendered. Even in slapstick cartoons good lessons can be taught. The main character overcomes setbacks and hardships to move on in life. This is not to say that the cartoons are *all* good. But they *do* have some principles you can capitalize on — if you are there.

3. Be a good example. Children learn by imitation, so limit your viewing hours and use your time creatively.

4. Replace TV viewing with an activity shared with your children. You are much more important to your child than is the TV. But you must take the initiative to be more exciting.

You can conduct an interesting experiment at home. Simply lock the TV set away in a closet and stop viewing it completely for one month. At first you might be bored and not know what to do with your time. Your children may whine and complain. But after a few days you will find other things to do. Get your news from the radio and newspaper. You will notice that you can get more done and feel more productive without the TV at all. Your children will become more resourceful and imaginative in finding activities and projects. The TV set is not a modern necessity; it is simply a plug-in drug to which many of us are addicted.

SUMMARY

The best way for you to help your children become better readers is to read to them. Almost everyone enjoys being read to. It simply depends on the time, place, and subject matter. Conversing about the story being read is very important because it conveys to the child that reading is more than just decoding words; it is about finding meaning and gaining insight. Television is the mortal enemy of reading and must be kept under tight control. In both increasing your child's reading and decreasing his TV viewing, an important ingredient is that you be a good example and model what you want him to do: Decrease watching TV and start reading.

Anchoring Questions for Chapter Eleven:

1. What will you teach your child about the importance of reading in his life?

2. How will you model the importance of reading?

3. What reading habits does your child exhibit for which you can encourage him?

You Can Have Quality Family Time

Navigating Principle #12: Every family needs a place and a time to prepare for navigating each week.

One way to spend quality time together as a family is to have a "family night." Family night is an evening when the entire family agrees to meet for prayer, Scripture reading, a topical study, and fellowship. A family night should be held on the same night each week and run from 6 to 9 P.M. or if you have younger children, it could go from 6 to 8 P.M. The main thing is that you devote an entire evening to being together as a family at least once a week.

The Bible tells us to "train up a child in the way he should go." That implies a plan, a format, a training schedule. Your family night should be designed to promote family unity, instruct the family in truth, open communication within the family, pray together, integrate what is learned at church and from the Bible with school and home life, and to have fun together.

Just because you live under the same roof and are biologically related does not guarantee a close family. Closeness is something for which you must work. All around each family there are elements that can pull it apart. Job, school, friends, and negative social influences all threaten the tight bond that should be found in the family. As our world becomes more hectic, we must fight harder for intimacy and connectedness. Creating a special time together may be just what you need in the midst of your busy schedule. A family time together need not occur in the evening. You may find that Saturday morning or Sunday afternoon are better times.

GOALS OF THE FAMILY TIME

You should have goals for this special family time together. It means more than simply spending time together. You need to establish what it is you hope to accomplish with your time together. This is not to bring pressure on you or your kids. Instead, it will give you a sense of direction and purpose and you will be able to look back on your family's steady growth.

The study of God's Word together as a family will emphasize to your children that God has expectations for each of us. The family can learn together what those divine expectations are and how to live up to them each week. This special time together also provides a wonderful time to share joys and disappointments in an environment of loving support.

A father who went through the *Charting* seminar later told me that he really didn't think the family night idea would work with his teenagers. He explained that he announced to his kids that the family was just going to meet together for thirty minutes each week and talk about what was happening in each other's lives. He also told them he would only require this for four weeks. Much to his surprise, when the kids started opening up and sharing what problems, concerns, and interests they had, their thirty-minute talk continued for three hours.

"It was fantastic," he told me. "We *really* talked!"

Another important goal of the family time together is that children learn how to deal with problems as a part of normal growth. As each person shares what is going on at work, at church, or at school the other members can share ideas and possible solutions. Your kids will see how you think through hardships and struggles and apply biblical thinking to everyday life. Of course, there may be certain problems with which you do not want to burden your children. Judgment is necessary for knowing just how much to reveal. But you are doing your children a disservice if you try to conceal all your struggles from them. They will be deprived of learning from your example.

Family night is also important for integrating what your children learn in the home with school, the church, and the Bible. We do not live our lives in separate compartments. Everything relates to everything else. During this time of family discussion this integration can be brought out.

A TYPICAL FORMAT

A very effective format for family night has seven main steps:

1. *Start promptly.* Have everyone gather in the living or family room, each with a Bible. Starting exactly on time sends a strong message that this time is important. One person opens with prayer.

2. Take turns *reading portions of the chosen Scripture* selection for that night.

3. Follow the reading with a *discussion* of the passage and its relevance to today. Steps one through three should take only thirty minutes. If you want to turn your children into atheists, spend the entire evening on Bible study. They will come to resent it.

4. *Discuss an issue* that is happening at school, a current event, or a family problem. Have everyone take turns and share what is going on in their lives. Empha-

size being courteous to each other. Allow only one person at a time to speak with no interruptions. This sharing time can be fun and lighthearted as well as serious. It may be good to risk a little and share a fear or worry you have about work or something of that nature. This is not to transmit instability to your children, but to let them see how you work through the problem. Putting on the mask of being the invincible parent, in the long run, will not help your children learn how to deal with tough issues. On the other hand, showing too much weakness to your children may erode their confidence in you altogether. They need to know they can rely on their parents for guidance and strength. Striking a balance here is important.

5. *Share your goals, plans, and successes.* During this time have each family member review his or her goals and report progress or obstacles. Be willing to let your children hold you accountable for your commitments. This is the time to lavish praise and offer encouragement to each other.

6. Everyone should talk about *specific prayer requests,* pray for each other, and join in worship. Many Christian families never pray together except before meals. Praying for specific needs is important for two reasons: God answers prayer and your children need to see you model being a prayer warrior.

7. Finally, adjourn to a *fun activity* such as a game or an outdoor activity. Avoid things that restrict family interaction such as going to the movies. This portion of the evening should take a least an hour and possibly more time. Make the family the "in" place to be.

A planned family night is a good way to be sure that you are spending quality time with your children. You need to be committed to it in order for it to be meaningful. Dr. Bob Simonds, the president of the National Association of Christian Educators/Citizens for Excellence in Education has actually cut business trips short and flown home early to be on time for his family night.

RESULTS TO LAST A LIFETIME

To summarize, remember to have six main elements to your Family Night: FAMILY.

F = Fun. It should be a fun time, not a chore.

A = Activity. Have an activity that everyone can join in.

M = Manners. Never allow family sharing to make anyone angry.

I = Imagination. Use your imagination to come up with interesting and new ideas for activities and lessons.

L = Learning. Make each session a learning experience.

Y = Yearning. The family night should instill in your family a yearning for God and a desire to live for Him.

When a person takes a blank canvas and applies oil paints to create a magnificent painting, it is called artistry. When a person applies hammer and saw to a piece of wood to create a beautiful piece of furniture, it is called craftsmanship. When a person applies pen to paper and writes a moving poem, it is called genius. And when you apply the twelve navigating principles outlined in this book, you will be charting your family's course.

Anchoring Questions for Chapter Twelve:

1. What will you teach to your child regarding the importance of family time together?

2. How will you model the importance of a special family time?

3. What is your child doing to promote family unity and love for which you can encourage him?

To contact the author regarding workshops and speaking engagements, write to Eric Buehrer, P.O. Box 514, Lake Forest, CA 92630; (714) 586-KIDS.

To have a *Charting Your Family's Course* seminar in your church, write to: NACE, Box 3200, Costa Mesa, CA 92628; (714) 546-5931.

Personal and Group Study Guide

Before beginning your personal or group study of *Charting Your Family's Course,* **take time to read these introductory comments.**

If you are working through the study on your own, you may want to adapt certain sections (for example, the icebreakers), and record your responses to all questions in a separate notebook. You might find it more enriching or motivating to study with a partner with whom you can share answers or insights.

If you are leading a group, you may want to ask your group members to read each assigned chapter and work through the study questions before the group meets. This isn't always easy for busy adults, so encourage them with occasional phone calls or notes between meetings. Help members manage their time by pointing out how they can cover a few pages each day. Also have them identify a regular time of the day or week that they can devote to the study. They too may write their responses to the questions in notebooks.

Notice that each session includes the following features:

Session Topic—a brief statement summarizing the session.
Icebreaker—an activity to help group members get better acquainted with the session topic and/or with each other.
Group Discovery Questions—a list of questions to encourage individual discovery or group participation.
Personal Application Questions—an aid to applying the knowledge gained through study to one's personal living. (Note: These are important questions for group members to answer for themselves, even if they do not wish to discuss their responses in the meeting.)

Optional Activities—supplemental ideas that will enhance the study.
Prayer Focus—suggestions for turning one's learning into prayer.
Assignment—activities or preparation to complete prior to the next session.

Here are a few tips which can help you more effectively lead small group studies:

Pray for each group member, asking the Lord to help you create an open atmosphere where everyone will feel free to share with one another and you.
Encourage group members to bring their Bibles as well as their texts to each session. This study guide is based on the *New International Version*, but it is good to have several translations on hand for purposes of comparison.
Start and end on time. This is especially important for the first meeting because it will set the pattern for the rest of the sessions.
Begin with prayer, asking the Holy Spirit to open hearts and minds and to give understanding so that truth will be applied.
Involve everyone. As learners, we retain only 10 percent of what we hear; 20 percent of what we see; 65 percent of what we hear and see; but 90 percent of what we hear, see, and do.
Promote a relaxed environment. Arrange the chairs in a circle or semicircle. This allows eye contact among members and encourages dynamic discussion. Be relaxed in your own attitude and manner. Be willing to share yourself.

1 Living Your Life on Purpose

Session Topic Because kids encounter so much mediocrity in school and society, parents must chart a course of achievement for them through teaching, modeling and encouraging.

Icebreakers (Choose one)

1. If you were to characterize your family life as an ocean-going vessel, which description would you choose:

a. Tight ship, smooth sailing!
b. Navigation system needs adjustment.
c. Who's the captain around here?
d. Keep bailing, everybody!
e. Abandon ship!

Share your response with the group and explain it. If possible, give an example to illustrate your choice.

2. The author gives two experiential definitions of contentment: Contentment is "being in the groove"; contentment is "running on all eight cylinders." As a parent, what would your experiential definition of contentment be? Why? (Note: experiential definitions use action words.)

Group Discovery Questions

1. What is the proportion of a child's time spent in school compared to time at home?
2. How much can a school do to help a child succeed? In what ways do public schools tend to fall short?
3. The author speaks of the rising tide of mediocrity in the schools. Can you cite any examples of this in your own child's experience? Any examples of challenges to excellence in the schools?
4. What is your reaction to Josh McDowell's survey about the condition of our young people? Would you say

you were more optimistic or pessimistic about the state
of things before reading this?
5. How would you define the word *underachiever?*
6. How does your definition compare with the author's?
Would you add any items to the underachiever characteristics listed?
7. In light of Proverbs 22:6, how would you describe the
difference between teaching and training? What new insights does the author give you about this?

Personal Application Questions
1. Would you say you are living your life more "by accident" or more "on purpose"? Explain.
2. What could you begin doing to maintain a better balance between: (1) your desire for academic excellence in
your child, and (2) your desire to improve his or her self
esteem? How can the two work together?
3. How would you describe your own children in relation
to the underachiever characteristics listed by the author?
4. How much "telling" do you give your child compared
to "training"? What next small step could you take to
build more training into the relationship?
5. What evidence do you have that your children look up
to you? How does this make you feel?
6. In what ways is your child already living out some of
the principles suggested in this chapter? Make a list of
these good qualities/actions in your children to help you
in your goal of encouraging them in the future.

Optional Activities
1. Create a chart of key events in your personal life history under two column-headings: On Purpose and Acci-
dental. When finished, review the chart and ask yourself:
*How has God's leading been evident in my life journey?
When has this been most clear? What changes in my
approach to life-planning would I like to make, starting
now?*
2. On a scale of 1 to 10, how would you rate your perfor-

mance in the three crucial areas of navigating children toward success—teaching, modeling, encouraging? Jot down one thing you could do under each category to help you improve your rate during the next 12 weeks.

Prayer Focus
Ask God to help you pay close attention to your children's needs in the coming weeks. Be open to learning ways to meet those needs with loving encouragement.

Assignment
1. Read Chapter 2.
2. Meditate on the following Scriptures and jot down some notes about how they relate to the theme of self-image: Ephesians 1:11; 2 Corinthians 5:19; 1 Peter 1:18; Colossians 3:4; Ephesians 2:18; Ephesians 2:4; Philippians 2:13; Psalm 37:23-24; James 5:15-16.

2 Boost Your Child's Self-image Biblically

Session Topic A healthy relationship with God leads to a strong self-image and clear life purpose.

Icebreaker

Each group member needs two index cards (for example, one white and one blue). Write down one thing "I'm Good At" on the white index card; on the blue card, jot down something "I'm No Good At." Then place all cards in a pile and shuffle them. As you read the cards aloud, try to guess who wrote them. Eventually, take turns answering this question: *Did anyone else think you were good at something you said you were no good at?*

Group Discovery Questions

1. The author points out that we tend to listen to what other people say about us more than we listen to God's words about us. Why does it seem so easy to do this?

2. Summarize the author's point about the Christian's typical response to doctrinal study ("product" vs. "perspective"). How does doctrine relate to self-esteem?

3. React to this statement in the text: "Self-image is intimately linked to achievement." What does the statement mean? Does it ring true in your experience? In your child's?

4. What two primary doctrinal facts about our relationship with God—two things God did—stand out as the keys to developing a healthy self-image?

5. Read 1 Samuel 16:7, Psalm 139:14, and John 7:24. What is a Christian "antidote" to a focus on mere physical attractiveness?

6. Respond to the author's statement that Christians are not required to just use their talents in specifically Christian endeavors. Do you agree or disagree? Should a writer who is a Christian be a "Christian writer"? What about a musician who is a Christian?

7. The author states that at the cross, God "proved our worthlessness." What did he mean? How does this relate to the ways in which God has shown us our value?

8. Why is it a "faulty assumption that if a person feels good about himself he will act virtuously"? Give an example from your parenting experience.

Personal Application Questions

1. How would you describe your relationship with God, based on the author's three categories: hostile, healthy, intimate? Explain.

2. How do you feel, being a "member of the Royal family"? Give an example of a practical difference this view of yourself could make in daily life.

3. Summarize the quotation by Dr. William Backus in your own words. What evidence do you have from your own experience of the truth of his statement?

4. In what particular ways does the personal reticular activating system hinder you or your child from trying new things or seeing yourself as potentially successful in certain activities? What could you do to change your mind's "gatekeeper" in this area?

5. Can you relate to the author's story about his period of dissatisfaction? Have you, too, ever wanted to "be somewhere else"? How did you deal with this desire?

Optional Activities

1. Divide into pairs or small buzz groups to discuss the Scriptures listed under "What God Says About You." Answer the question: *In what specific ways could applying these passages contribute to a Christian's self-esteem?* You may wish to list responses on newsprint and evaluate them together as a large group.

2. If you were to receive a report card on your performance in relation to the Five Great Truths, how would you do? Grade yourself on each one by putting one of the following letters next to each of the numbered points in the text: O (outstanding); S (satisfactory); N (needs im-

provement). What are your insights on how your
"grades" affect your personal success development (see
the four stages of success development)?
3. As participants call out responses, jot items on newsprint or chalkboard under this heading: Things We Have
Been Given in Salvation. The author begins such a list
on page 30.

Prayer Focus
Read Psalm 8, then spend some moments in praise and
thankfulness for God's wonderful creation—including
you!

Assignment
1. Read Chapter 3.
2. Consider: *How much affirmation did I receive as a
child? How much affirmation do I give to my own
children?*

3 Define Biblical Success for Your Child

Session Topic We attain true success as we develop internal qualities of character, using our abilities according to the life purpose God has given us.

Icebreaker

How would you define success? Pretend you are one of the people below and write a one-sentence definition of success from the perspective of the role you have chosen:
- Your next-door neighbor
- A teenage gang member
- Your child's teacher
- Your child
- Your spouse
- Your minister
- A yuppie
- A street person
- Your boss

Discuss: *What qualities do you find in common in your definitions? What basic human needs are people struggling to meet when they strive for success?*

Group Discovery Questions

1. Why can't success be measured by subjective experience alone? What other factor(s) must be considered?
2. How would you characterize the difference between momentary success and lifestyle success? What are some advantages and disadvantages of each?
3. In what ways does the word *potential* tend to highlight failure rather than success? If possible, give an example from your own childhood. What better, alternative word could we think of in relation to our children's activities?
4. What is the "point" of the Eagles and Eels anecdote? How would you sum it up in just one sentence?
5. Where does the greatest battle for the lifestyle of success occur? Why?

Personal Application Questions

1. Paraphrase the author's definition of success in your own words. How does this definition compare to the one

you have used (consciously or unconsciously) in your life
so far? How does it compare to the one you tend to use
with your children?

2. What is your "method" for discerning God's guidance? Read Proverbs 3:5-6. How have you learned to deal
with the two entities here: (1) your own understanding;
(2) acknowledging God in all your ways? How might
those two entities compete? How might they work
together?

3. What is your reaction to this statement by the author:
"Children are often most unlovable when they need love
the most." Do you agree? How do you tend to respond at
those times? How could you start responding more
lovingly?

4. How would you evaluate the "affirmation environment" of your household (the amount of affirmation that
is given and received among family members)? Circle the
number that best describes the environment:

1   **2**   **3**   **4**   **5**

Barren Desert   Tropical Paradise

5. Now circle the number above that best describes the
"affirmation environment" of your childhood household.
In what ways are you, as a parent, carrying on the legacy
of your own parents in this area? Is this good or bad?

6. How did you feel when you read about the person who
"peaked out in the 9th grade"? In what areas have you
settled for momentary achievement while paying less attention to lifestyle achievement?

7. The author tells about his friend's driving pursuit of
business and athletic success. What similar experiences
have you had in which you got to the top and said, "Is
this all there is?" What have you learned from those
experiences? What advice could you offer your children
as a result?

8. What did you learn from plotting your child's present
character qualities, as suggested by the author (p. 51)?

What does this exercise indicate to you about areas for future work toward change?

Optional Activities

1. Set up a "revolving panel" of three or four participants who will share various methods they have used to help affirm their children. When the panel has given its ideas and taken some questions, ask another panel to form and do the same.

2. On a sheet of paper, repeat the exercise under "Locating Your Child's Present Position." But this time ask yourself: *How would my parents evaluate me?* Fill out the chart from this perspective. Then think: *What are my insights about the qualities I am equipped to convey to my children?*

Prayer Focus

Review the characteristics of lifestyle achievers. Ask God to help you restructure your definition of success to include qualities of "being" rather than just "doing."

Assignment

1. Read Chapter 4.

2. Ponder these questions during the coming week: *How do I know what is right and wrong? What other systems of morality challenge my starting point for ethical decision-making?*

4 Navigate Life's Reefs with God's Moral Compass

Session Topic Because living ethically requires more than just knowing how to make decisions, Christians strive for moral development in their children based on revealed absolutes.

Icebreakers *(Choose one)*
1. Do you agree or disagree with the following statements? As the group leader reads each one aloud, raise your hand if you agree. Then go back and explain or clarify your responses.
   - Emotion should play no part in moral decisions.
   - All truth is God's truth.
   - Morality is never situational.
   - Children will learn values more by example than precept.
   - Since there are moral absolutes, ethical decision-making is not required.

2. Choose one of the sentences below and write a phrase to complete it. Then share with the group your responses to the three questions.

"My earliest recollection of a moral decision that I made was when . . ."
or:
"The last time I had to make a significant moral decision was when . . ."

   - Tell what happened.
   - Tell what values influenced your decision.
   - Tell what method of decision-making you used.

Group Discovery Questions
1. What is wrong with the popular idea that parents and teachers should not impose values but wait for children

to choose for themselves?

2. Evaluate and critique the seven decision-making factors used in Values Clarification courses. In what ways are they used by all decision-makers, even Christians?

3. According to the author, what are the two major shortcomings of these seven factors?

4. What does the author mean by: "Being a moral person often means not looking at any alternatives"? Do you agree with this statement? Explain.

5. What was the author's point in quoting Plato?

6. "You don't 'figure out' morality, you *learn* it." Your reaction? What is the place of "figuring out" in a Christian's moral decision-making process?

Personal Application Questions

1. The author says we *demonstrate* values more than we *explain* values. What examples can you cite in which your children detected a difference between what you said and what you did? What could you do differently to keep this from happening again?

2. What is your personal assessment of Values Clarification philosophy and methods?

3. Have you clearly thought through your own "philosophy of decision-making" as a Christian? Describe it as clearly and succinctly as possible.

4. What are your reasons for holding to the existence of moral absolutes? Suppose someone says: "But you have chosen the Bible as your moral standard just like everyone else chooses a standard for themselves. All such choices are arbitrary." How might you respond?

5. How realistic would it be, in your particular situation, to try to "win the teacher over," as the author suggests? How might you proceed?

6. What stories, from the Bible and from secular literature, come to mind as providing good examples of moral virtue? How familiar are your children with these stories?

7. Has your child assumed a moral core? How do you

know? Can you give an example related to a recent decision your child has made?

Optional Activities

1. Assign one of the letters in the M-O-R-A-L-S acrostic to individuals, partners, or small groups for a period of brainstorming. The task of each group is to answer: *What practical ideas can we develop that would aid the practice of this principle in a typical family?* Regather, share and discuss the ideas.

2. In advance, have one of your group members prepare a report on the various systems of ethics. The reporter could consult any standard "Intro to Philosophy" college textbook. After the report, discuss the merits of a "Divine Command" system in relation to the other systems described.

Prayer Focus

Ask the Holy Spirit to make you more aware of rationalizations you use to continue wrong behavior. Spend some time praising God, too, for areas of evident moral growth in you and your children.

Assignment

1. Read Chapter 5.
2. Jot down some short-term and long-term goals you have been working toward.

5 Chart Your Family's Course with Goal-Setting

Session Topic Goal-setting gives evidence of the self-discipline required for consistent achievement.

Icebreakers *(Choose one)*

1. Survey participants about their eating habits: (1) Who sometimes eats dessert first? (2) Who saves the "best" part of the meal for last? (3) How do you eat a sandwich cookie—middle first, last, or all together?

Notice that children often practice delayed gratification through their eating habits, sometimes "saving the best for last." Discuss: *What are some adult versions of this? Why is it important to learn the discipline required to delay gratification?*

2. Share your most important short-term goal right now. What are some key long-term goals? How would you characterize yourself as a goal setter? Are you a:

- Pre-plan Penelope?
- Organized Oscar?
- Meticulous Martha?
- Denny Disarray?
- Laid-back Larry?
- Float-along Frieda?

Explain your choice to the rest of the group members.

Group Discovery Questions

1. What is the author's advice about how to stimulate your child's will to achieve?
2. How would you describe the relationship between God's *government* of our lives and our *management* of our lives?
3. Many young people grow up wanting rewards. But what have they often failed to realize about how to get such rewards?

4. How can goal-setting help a child have more sense of power and control in his or her life? Do you have any examples from your parenting experience?

5. What is the relationship between goal-setting and leadership?

6. Name the author's three broad guidelines for goal-setting. What key reasons are given for each one? Jot these down, then discuss them together.

Personal Application Questions

1. How often do you encourage your children to think about what they want and how they want to achieve those things?

2. When have you felt things were "not going according to plan"? Think: *Was* there a plan at the time?

3. Read Deuteronomy 6:5. What might be considered the highest life-achievement goal to aim for? How would accomplishing this goal "look" in your life? Your child's life? Make a list of daily steps to take to move toward that goal.

4. What would it mean for you to be a good role-model of a close walk with God? Share about a specific life situation in which you have tried to do this. How did it go?

5. The author points out that many people don't set goals due to the risk of failure. How would you rate yourself on the "Fear of Failure Scale" below:

1	2	3	4	5
Scared Stiff				Ready to Try
"I'll just die				"I'll just learn
if I fail."				from mistakes."

6. What is the difference between a dream and a goal? Who is your favorite example of someone who was able to turn a dream into a goal and accomplish it? Consider sharing this story with your child.

7. In your opinion, what are some key next steps to take in helping your child cross the bridge from external discipline to internal discipline?

Optional Activities

1. Think of areas of personal success or specific accomplishments. Share about the planning (or lack of it) that preceded those accomplishments. In light of this sharing, discuss the author's comments on the necessity of goal-setting for achievement, for example: "Achievement rarely happens by accident."

2. Make a chart with three column-headings:

DREAMS	GOALS	STEPS TOWARD GOALS

Jot down some of your dreams and some of your goals. What specific steps could you take to turn one or more of your dreams into an attainable goal? Jot these steps in the third column and get feedback from other group members about your plans.

Prayer Focus

Study Philippians 1:6. Praise God for His intention to finish the work He has started within you. Ask Him for greater insight into His daily goals for you.

Assignment

1. Read Chapter 6.
2. Make a list of the most important areas of your life. Contemplate your level of satisfaction with how things are going in those areas.

6 Voyage Full Speed Ahead with Your Family

Session Topic Through a process of self-evaluation and patient consideration of where we want to be, we can set goals for ourselves in the 10 major areas of life.

Icebreakers *(Choose one)*
1. Do a word association exercise. What thoughts or impressions first come to mind when you hear the words below? (As you read each one, respond with your first impression.)

> *goals*
> *recreation*
> *school*
> *television*
> *family togetherness*
> *money*
> *character*
> *vocation*

2. Consider this mini-case: Mary had just read a self-help book about "Getting Your Act Together." It contained a detailed plan to transform her personal life and her family life. But she got up on the next Monday morning and realized she faced the same dull routine of work, parenting, and homemaking. *Actually,* she thought, *it's all I can do just to get through a day without a major crisis. How am I supposed to do all this transforming stuff? It's depressing!*

Be Mary's friend. Can you relate to her feelings? What advice would you give her?

Group Discovery Questions
1. The author states that having a specific direction in life is essential. How would you relate this idea to Jesus' teaching about "taking no thought for tomorrow"? (Matthew 6:34)

2. Developing goals in the 10 life areas, all at once, could seem overwhelming. What method is suggested in the text to avoid this problem?
3. What do you think the author meant by: "Avoid making the means an end in itself"? How does this statement apply to setting goals for spiritual growth?
4. What are some ways we could respond to the problem that "many children take for granted our form of government"?
5. Do you believe it is better to see ourselves as "inhabitants" of the world rather than "citizens" of the world? What are some implications of this distinction for goal-setting in the area of citizenship?
6. What are the roles of the school and the parent in a biblical concept of education? Refer to Deuteronomy 6:6-7 in your response.
7. React to this statement by the millionaire: "Generosity is the only thing that will break the bondage of money in your life."

Personal Application Questions
1. The author says it is important to start goal-setting by determining where you want to be spiritually. How do you respond to his suggested question: "Specifically, where is my life lacking, and how do I want to be"?
2. List some of the major obstacles to family togetherness in your household. Jot down some possible solutions or adjustments to family routines that could help overcome them? Think: What steps could I take to start practicing the author's suggestion to "make family togetherness a top priority"?
3. What would be the best way for you to get the whole family involved in goal-setting? How would you go about this? List some of the steps required.
4. What areas of self-education have you helped your child pursue in the last year?
5. What is your current avocation? If you do not have one, list two or three things you'd like to try in the

future. List some things you have noticed your child
showing interest in, too.
6. How well would the idea of restricted access to the TV
go over in your family? What benefits might such a policy
bring to your family?

Optional Activities
1. Divide into pairs or small groups and brainstorm family togetherness ideas. What has worked for you in the
past? What ideas could you incorporate from others'
experiences?
2. Develop "child definitions" of the key financial terms
listed in the text (the definitions would have to be under-
standable to a kindergartner). Then discuss the best
ways to introduce children to financial responsibility.
3. Distribute construction paper, scissors, and markers.
Assign one or more of the 10 life areas to individuals or
small groups. Each person or group should create a
bumper sticker that summarizes the key point under the
assigned text subhead representing a life area.

Prayer Focus
Ask God to give you the patience to start with one area of
improvement—and to stick with it. Thank Him that He
promises to supply the time and energy to accomplish the
things that really matter.

Assignment
1. Read Chapter 7.
2. Contemplate this question during the week: "What
good things about my child and her performance have I
been taking for granted?"

7 Discover Buried Treasure in Your Child

Session Topic Children thrive on affirmation and encouragement.

Icebreakers *(Choose one)*

1. Do a graffiti poster. Tape a large poster board or piece of newsprint to one wall before your session begins. At the top, write: ENCOURAGEMENT IS. . . . As group members arrive, they can complete the statement as they wish. Be creative—use words, statements, pictures, symbols. Later, ask: *What's the best thing about receiving an encouraging word?* Share about the last encouragement you received at work or at home.

2. Have a "praise party." Divide into pairs for one-minute interviews to find out *the one most praiseworthy thing* about a person or his activities during the past week. Then partners introduce one another, after which the person introduced receives an enthusiastic round of applause. Discuss: How does applause feel to you? Name an instance of 'applause' (praise or encouragement) you received as a child. Why is it so memorable?

Group Discovery Questions

1. Why is a treasure hunt story such an appropriate way to begin a chapter on encouragement?

2. What are two basic sources of motivation in a child's life (the need to _____ and the need for _____)? In what ways have you seen these needs come through in your own child? Share.

3. What does the author mean by "cycle of failure"? What are his suggestions for avoiding this cycle?

4. Is encouragement an art or a science? Explain.

5. React to the quote by Charles Schwab about working better in an approval environment. Can you verify the truth of his statement with an example from your own experience?

6. Describe the difference between focusing on *who a child is* compared to *how a child performs*. Why is the distinction important?
7. What is the difference between ordinary encouragement and specifically Christian encouragement? Refer to Ephesians 3:16-17, 20 in your response.

Personal Application Questions

1. Have you ever thought of your child as containing buried treasure? Make a list of some of your child's "golden" qualities.
2. In light of your list, would you say you are supplying adequate amounts of encouragement? Make another list of affirmations you have given your child in the last week.
3. How do you react to the statement by Carnegie about looking for gold in employees? Where would you put yourself on this Treasure Detector scale with regard to your children?

1 _____ 2 _____ 3 _____ 4 _____ 5
Tend to   Tend to
look for dirt   look for gold

4. What change of attitude and/or habits would need to occur in your approach for you to pay more attention to catching your child being good than to catching him or her being bad?
5. Recall the three-step encouraging technique and jot down an instance of your child's behavior from the past week that deserves affirmation. Write a three-point encouraging sentence you could say to your child about the behavior.
6. "A parent who does everything for a child teaches that child to be powerless." In what areas could you help empower your child by doing a little *less* for him or her? Take one concrete step in that direction this week.

Optional Activities

1. Spend some time practicing the three-step encouraging technique. Form pairs or teams. Each team should make up a situation calling for affirmation or encouragement of a child. Other group members will then role play a specific three-point statement that could be spoken to the child.

2. As an optional closing activity, consider exchanging Affirmation Memos. Distribute paper and pencils and write a brief paragraph in complicated, technical business jargon. The point is to affirm someone in the group regarding one of his or her "golden" qualities. (Example: MEMO: Pursuant to my most recent conversation with you, and in light of your uncompromising attention to detail, be advised that you are an outstanding listener.")

Prayer Focus

Ask God to open your eyes to the good qualities in your children.

Assignment

1. Read Chapter 8.
2. Make a list of expectations you have for your child.

8 Empower Your Child through Expectations

Session Topic Raising our expectations for our children raises their levels of success.

Icebreakers *(Choose one)*
1. Have you ever experienced a self-fulfilling prophecy? Tell about your most memorable instance of this. Share: *How does your experience relate to the theme of this chapter?*
2. Do an acrostic of the word E-X-P-E-C-T. Distribute index cards and have group members jot down as many entries for each letter as possible. Later, as a group, decide on the best word choice for each letter. Then debate this proposition: "As long as we feel good about ourselves, failure and success are not that important."

Group Discovery Questions
1. In your opinion, do we live too much or too little according to others' expectations? When is it helpful and when is it unhelpful to let expectations spur us to achievement? How do your responses relate to the performance of your children?
2. How do the ways we refer to one another affect performance?
3. The author says that our expectations help determine how our children will respond to their tasks. But what effect do our expectations for our children have on *us?*
4. What steps beyond "baseball chatter" must we take to make expectations truly affirming and effective?
5. Suppose your teacher says, "A child's self-esteem is damaged when we expect too much." How would you respond?
6. What, according to the author, do teenagers crave more than freedom? Do you agree? Explain, with reference to the anecdote about the teacher's sex education poll.

Personal Application Questions

1. In what ways do you pattern your life around expectations? Think of some specific instances in your life and in your child's.
2. "The Bible emphasizes hating the sin but loving the sinner." How does this principle apply to your current parenting methods? Give a specific example of when you used it.
3. How do your children refer to one another? Is there any name-calling that needs to be curtailed? How do *you* refer to your children?
4. Make a list of "innocent" but potentially damaging names you have heard parents calling their children.
5. What do the results of the international math testing say to you about the state of American education? What changes would you recommend to teachers if you were a school superintendent?
6. What have you done to prepare your children for the public school's approach to sex education?

Optional Activities

1. Make a master list of typical parental comments that can cause children to "live down" to expectations. Work on changing the comments to encouraging statements. Use two columns on a chalkboard or newsprint to help you:

LIVE DOWN TO   *LIVE UP TO*
"Why do you always   "I appreciate how you
have to. . . .   always. . . ."

2. Do a group Bible Search. Distribute Bibles and concordances and allow time for group members to find biblical examples of "Hating the sin, but loving the sinner." Take turns reading the discovered passages aloud and discussing present-day applications.
3. Through discussion, develop a possible approach to sex education for Christian parents. You may wish to

appoint someone (in advance) to do a brief report on the
approach currently used in the local public schools.

Prayer Focus
Praise God for His high expectations that come through
in the Scriptures. Then thank Him for the person and
work of Christ, who meets every demand on our behalf,
calling us to respond with gratitude and holy living.

Assignment
1. Read Chapter 9.
2. Make a list of all the things you've done that seemed
like failures at one time but that turned out later to be
preludes to success.

9 Orchestrate Success in Your Child's Life

Session Topic Helping children have small successes prepares them to bounce back from future failures.

Icebreakers *(Choose one)*

1. Athletes speak of "choking" on a play—being paralyzed by the fear of failure to the point of causing themselves to miss the shot or make a bad throw. Ask: *Who can share about a personal instance of choking in a sports contest? What is the cure for this phenomenon? What does it mean to choke in life?*

2. Distribute paper and pencils and do "Success/Failure Personal History Time Lines." Draw a line across the paper and mark dates of significant successes and (what you might have considered) significant failures in your life. Share a little bit about your time line with others in your group. Discuss: *In what cases have you found failure to be a prelude, or even a stimulus, to future success?*

Group Discovery Questions

1. Explain the differences among these three: (1) letting your child win artificially; (2) manipulating your child toward success; (3) orchestrating success by creating an "achievement environment."

2. Complete this sentence from the text: "Nothing stimulates the desire for success more than the _____."

3. What did Zig Ziglar mean by: "Knowing how to benefit from failures is the key to success"?

4. What benefits can frustration provide for us and our children? Refer to the psychiatrist's statement in your response.

5. With books closed, as a group, recall the eight listed symptoms of a learning disability. How would you respond to a teacher who called a child with these symptoms "just a big discipline problem"?

6. What point was the author making by quoting 1 Timothy 1:15-16? How would you state this point in a sentence of 10 words or less?

7. Why is "achievement no guarantee of happiness"? Is there any *guarantee* of happiness in life? Share your insights about this.

8. List some of the dangers of comparing your child with others.

Personal Application Questions

1. Do an "orchestrating success process" related to one of your child's interests, according to the author's description of the process on page 121. What would you need to do to keep this from being manipulative in any way?

2. How have you handled failure in your life in the past? What instances can you point to in which your failure served to pave the way for a future success? Determine to share this experience with your child.

3. How do your children handle failure? How is their ability to deal with failure related to what they see in your own past performance?

4. What evidences of "learned helplessness" do you find in your children?

5. Do a personal inventory to discover what legitimate expectations you hold for your child and what self-fantasies you may be imposing on them. Use two columns to better see the differences:

I want for my child:

LEGITIMATE EXPECTATIONS	UNREALISTIC FANTASIES

6. Review the five common sources of failure. Are your children experiencing any of these problems? If so, what specific plan of action do you have for remedying these problems? Jot down the next step to take.
7. Which of the myths of success would you say "hits closest to home" in your family? Why?

Optional Activities
1. Have a period of silence in which adults can fill out the checklists for determining reasons for a child's failure (see pages 127 and 128). After a time of personal reflection, have volunteers share insights and/or reveal specific prayer requests.
2. Divide the group into three smaller groups and assign each group one of the Myths of Success. The groups' task is to develop a countering Truth of Success (as opposed to "myth") based on biblical principles. Encourage group members to search the Scriptures to find verses, passages or Bible character examples that back up their truth statements. Then discuss specific parenting applications.

Prayer Focus
Ask God to help you reinterpret past failures as learning experiences and opportunities for renewed spiritual growth.

Assignment
1. Read Chapter 10.
2. Make a list of the ways your child may find your home to be a place of refuge from his or her problems.

10 Build a Safe Harbor for Your Child at Home

Session Topic Creating a home environment of success is like offering your child a safe harbor from the storms of life.

Icebreakers *(Choose one)*

1. What experiences have you had of "coming in from the cold," or coming into safety after a trial of endurance? Share about that. Discuss: *How is a child's coming home from school similar to these experiences of finding refuge?*

2. Invite personal testimonies of group members' conversion experiences. How is salvation like reaching a safe harbor?

Group Discovery Questions

1. What are the two saddest words in life (according to Zig Ziglar)? How can they be exchanged for happy words?

2. How could a family ministries pastor end up having no time for his family? What recommendations would you make in that situation?

3. Describe the difference between dialogue and monologue. What are some benefits of dialogue with your children?

4. Give examples of both ineffective and effective questions that could be asked of a child when he or she arrives home from school.

5. Compare and contrast the effect on children (in your opinion) of playing TV video games with the effect of reading books.

6. What are the two basic academic subjects that can be applied to any area of interest? Tell, specifically, how they can be used to increase academic success.

7. React to this statement from the text: "Education is learning what to do with a living *after* you earn it." How does it apply to your own experience with education?

Personal Application Questions

1. How do you respond to the country philosopher's statement: "The best inheritance parents can give their children is—a few minutes of their time each day."

2. How does the amount of time you spend with your children compare to the national average given in the text?

3. How much intimate conversation takes place among your family members? Name one or more things you have learned about your child through his or her sharing during a conversation?

4. List five good questions to ask your child when he comes home from school.

5. What are your initial impressions about what your learning style might be? Your child's? What adjustments in your approach to your children's education might you make after reading about learning styles?

6. What subject areas that your child is studying would you like to learn more about? Name one. Would you consider going to the library to check out books on the subject that you and your child could discuss together?

Optional Activities

1. Do an inventory of personal "If only's" you have, related to your interaction with your children. Then think about specific plans you could carry out "next time." Use the columns below to jot your notes:

IF ONLY	NEXT TIME

2. Have group members think back through this day and do a chart, according to the author's instructions, to show how they used their time. Share: *What are your insights about how you tend to use your time? What immediate ideas do you have about how to improve your efficiency?*

Prayer Focus
Thank God for the sense of peace and safety He gives in the midst of stormy life circumstances.

Assignment
1. Read Chapter 11.
2. Pick out a favorite book (a personal favorite or a child's favorite) that you could share with your group members at the next session.

11 How to Help Your Child Become a Better Reader

Session Topic Reading aloud to children produces in them a love for learning.

Icebreakers *(Choose one)*
1. Invite group members to consider the experience of being read to. What is it like? Read aloud to them for about ten minutes (how about a Mark Twain short story?) Discuss: How did it feel while being read to? Describe the "special pleasure" in the experience. How do you think children feel when parents read to them?
2. Divide into two teams and have a contest: "The TV vs. Bible Memory Challenge." One team member calls out a line from a TV commercial; the other team must then recite a Scripture verse. Do this until either side runs out of memory material. Who wins?

Group Discovery Questions
1. The author says there is an aspect of conditioning that takes place when we read to children. Explain.
2. How do you account for the amazing ability of the author, as a substitute teacher, to hold the attention of a class of high schoolers? Relate your response to your view about the importance of reading aloud to kids.
3. As a group, with books closed, recite four or five specific advantages of reading aloud to children. Share some instances in which you have seen these benefits displayed in your own experience of reading to children.
4. Could schools really be revolutionized through more reading aloud to children at home—as school superintendent Ruth Love once stated? Why, or why not?
5. What related activity seems to be just as important as the reading aloud itself? Why?
6. In what ways does TV demand instant adulthood from children? What are some potential problems with this?

Personal Application Questions

1. The author states that all children enjoy being read to. Have you found this to be the case with your own children? What are your reading-aloud plans for your children for the next week? Next month? Next three months?

2. How do you go about matching the right book with the right child? Make a list of books you'd like to read to your children during the coming year:

Child   *Type of Book Needed*   *Possible Title*

3. When could you schedule into your busy family life a time when everyone reads silently? What adjustments to routines would need to be made?

4. Recall the little girl who was shocked to find no TV in the host's home. Think creatively for a few moments: *What could your family do instead of watch TV?* Jot down some of your ideas and share the possibilities with other family members.

5. Spend a moment contemplating the author's closing statement: "The TV set is not a modern necessity, it is simply a plug-in drug to which we are addicted." Do you agree?

Optional Activities

1. After your "formal" class session time is over, consider sitting down together in front of the TV and watching any half-hour of programming (chosen at random). Critique and discuss what you saw: *What themes came through? What values were held up? What relationship*

*did the program have to Christian faith? In what ways
could the program be helpful to a child? Harmful? What
is the overall effect on character or spiritual growth?*
2. In advance, notify group members to bring a favorite
book with them to the session. The book could be a personal favorite or one they have found a child to enjoy.
Give each person a chance to do a very brief "show and
tell" with the book (or a mini-book report).

Prayer Focus
Ask God to give you the ability to put aside your own
"agenda" each day to make time for reading to your
children. That will be tough; but with God, all things are
possible!

Assignment
1. Read Chapter 12.
2. Review each of the 11 previous chapters, looking for
the one key point or thought that has been most helpful
to you in each.

12 You Can Have Quality Family Time

Session Topic A regular family time strengthens the bonds of closeness among family members while increasing mutual love and respect.

Icebreakers *(Choose one)*
1. Share with the group your fondest memory of a family time together. It can be recent, or from your childhood. Discuss: *What makes such times so special in our memories? What are some of the key characteristics of a "great" family time?*
2. Do a review activity using the first 11 of the 12 Navigating Principles listed at the end of the chapter. Assign one or more principles to individuals. They will have the task of skimming through the related chapters in order to prepare a one-minute (maximum) mini-report on the chapter's key points to give to the other group members.

Group Discovery Questions
1. How much time does the author recommend setting aside for a family night? Why might less than that be counterproductive?
2. "Closeness is something for which you must work." Do you agree with this statement? Why, or why not?
3. In what ways should a family night be more than "just spending time together"?
4. How would you (or do you) strike a balance between revealing your own struggles to your children and maintaining their confidence in you (and the stability of the family)?
5. What is the author's recommendation for the ratio of Bible study to fun activities in a fun night? What are his reasons for this ratio?
6. What ideas, from your own family experience, would you recommend adding to the author's family night suggestions? Share these with others in your group.

Personal Application Questions

1. What is your immediate reaction to the idea of a family night? How feasible does it seem for your family to set one up?

2. What would be the main roadblocks to setting up a family night? How could you get around these obstacles? Jot your thoughts in two columns:

ROADBLOCKS   POSSIBLE DETOURS

3. Have you found that "closeness is something for which you must work"? Think of a time when you felt especially close as a family. What "work" went into bringing that situation about? How might those circumstances and preparations be duplicated in the future? What are your specific ideas?

4. Could you envision cutting a business trip short in order to be on time for a family night? Why, or why not?

5. How about making an attempt to set up a regular family night? Fill in this preliminary planning chart for your first meeting:

Possible date: Time: Place:
Possible Activities:
Scripture:
Fun Activity:

Action steps required to arrange discussion with spouse and children:

1.
2.
3.
4.
5.
6.

Optional Activity

To bring a sense of closure to the ending of your course, you may wish to spend some time assessing what happened during your 12 or more weeks together. Share and discuss questions like these: *What did we gain/learn from this course? From being with each other in the group? What parts of the study were most helpful or life-changing? Did any part of this course fall below our expectations? What could have been done better? What affirmations do we wish to give one another before we depart?*

Also spend some time planning what the group wants to do now: Disband? Meet again for another study? Have a family picnic or potluck as a closing activity? Invite others into the group?

Prayer Focus

Ask God to help you follow through on implementing your plans for better family life in at least one area.